THE MARTIAL ARTIST'S WAY

THE MARTIAL ARTIST'S WAY

Achieve Your Peak Performance

by Sifu Glen Doyle

with Forewords by
Elvis Stojko and Bruce Burton

■ HarperCollins*PublishersLtd*

http://www.harpercanada.com

HarperCollins books may be purchased for educational, business, or sales promotional use. For information please write: Special Markets Department, HarperCollins Canada, 55 Avenue Road, Suite 2900, Toronto, Ontario M5R 3L2.

First edition

Canadian Cataloguing in Publication Data

Doyle, Glen, 1965-
The martial artist's way

ISBN 0-00-638583-4

1. Martial arts. 2. Martial arts - Philosophy. I. Title
GV1101.D694 1999   796.8   C98-932884-8

99 00 01 02 03 04 HC 10 9 8 7 6 5 4 3 2 1

Printed and bound in the United States

CONTENTS

"When it's too tough for everyone else…it's just right for me."

Gregory J. Doyle
1934–1998

Newfoundlander • Korea War Veteran • Iron Worker • Father

Dad,

Yours was the hand that taught me to throw my very first punch… And mine was the hand that held yours as you took your final breath.

I've still got some important work to do down here, dad. But when the 'Big Man' informs me I'm done, I'll see you again. And just remember… you still owe me one more lesson.

your son, Glen

ACKNOWLEDGMENTS

The author would like to thank first and foremost Sifu James Lore (Lore King Hong) of the Jing Mo Kung-Fu Club for his endless dedication to the teaching of both his fighting art and his culture. Without Sifu Lore's influence, many of the pages in this book would be empty or devoid of certainty. It is with a humble heart that the author says thank you. There would be no *Martial Artist's Way* without you, Sifu.

A definite thank you is warranted to Tuttle Publishing, who gave this book a chance. From the first manuscript submission to the final details of this publication, their professionalism was second to none.

And thank you to all those friends who believed and never lost their faith: Roque and Verna, Jason and Lisa, Stuart Webb and Dave "The Hammer" Schultz—you guys are awesome. To all the members of the Jing Mo Kung-Fu club, Dr. Jasper Sidhu, Suzanne Naughton, Jim (Dr. Bandoli) Ince, Robin Young, Jopet Laraya, and especially John Rivers, and Lanz Boglander... to all of you... your smiles had more power than you might believe.

To Sensei Sean Stewart and the students and instructors of the Ontario Center for Martial Arts: thank you for the use of your facilities and the donation of your time.

Acknowledgments

To photographer Jerry Riley, for answering the call when few would, and for putting all your efforts into each and every picture...a handshake and a thank you.

To sweet Roselle. Your eyes saw what I couldn't, and your spirit was strong when mine wasn't. Thank you...thank you for walking this road with me.

And finally to my mom...I love you ('nuff said).

Elvis Stojko

*Three-Time World Figure Skating Champion/
Martial Arts Enthusiast*

Physical and mental harmony has always been the focus of most athletes. Through practice, conditioning, and research, many have strived to prove themselves as icons in the sport of their choice. Numerous factors can challenge, aid, or encourage this journey as long as the guidance is true and beneficial. An athlete without a pathway is bound to fall from grace eventually.

Many aspects of the sporting world can lead athletes to the euphoria of their dreams, but, should they choose an unfavorable avenue in their sport, then feelings of both resentment and disinterest begin to take shape. So many times a gifted athlete will lose the edge because of a wrong decision or training procedure. It is this constant failing that has led many potential champions down the road of disappointment.

The martial arts, being a sport as well as a cultural identity, are no different in attitude and practice. The right decisions must be made to ensure proper growth, the right instructor must be chosen to guarantee a good learning etiquette, and a proper school must be chosen to ensure a healthy training environment. Within all of these factors are areas of thought and common sense—areas that, due to lack of either experience or confidence, get missed.

The Martial Artist's Way can help and assist in preventing all of these potential pitfalls. *The Martial Artist's Way* contains a very simple and modern look at this ancient art that works on all levels: for the beginner, it can make or break that critical first year of practice; for the intermediate, an aspect of refocusing or rediscovery can be achieved; and for the advanced or instructing practitioner, *The Martial Artist's Way* may help formulate new training approaches and teaching styles.

Training in two separate physical mediums (figure skating and the martial arts, for example) can sometimes tax the mind and body to a level that, in time, could become detrimental to performance in both sports. Having been trained by Glen Doyle,

I have had both the benefit of personal attention and, more importantly, the benefit of the simplicity of Glen's teaching style, which allows total freedom. My thoughts toward both training and practical application were guided from within, rather than having generic ideals forced upon me. This not only increased my martial arts ability, but gave me a drive and hunger to continue my exploration into these charismatic principles. Although Glen did not adhere solely to the "classical" way of teaching, I did learn all the classical foundations needed in order to progress.

Within the pages of *The Martial Artist's Way* you will not only be able to appreciate the personability of pure martial art education and instruction, but you will also learn to find, within yourself, the tools needed to achieve advancement in any sport, training, or practice.

Have Fun!
Elvis Stojko

Bruce Burton, BSc, MPA

National Level Coach (Track and Field)
Author of several articles a propos to training for sport

On the surface, this book is an attempt at guiding those interested in the martial arts: selecting the best school or club; attitude toward others; the training of the internal, as well as the external; and learning to focus knowledge towards proper and timely application. Those not involved in the ancient arts, however, should not dismiss its contents out-of-hand as being relevant only to a limited area. Rather, the message contained within these pages can be applied, by both coach and athlete, to any sport known to man.

One of the largest industries in the world is that of advertising. The core of a successful advertising campaign lies in the fact that people tend to look for the easy or popular answer to what they think they need (No, Virginia, you will not be spotted by Prince Charming across a crowded room based on your choice of chewing gum!). Consequently, people buy into products or programs without examining them closely—owning a fancy sports car is "cool," but the salesman doesn't tell you that repairs, which may be needed often, can only be done by a specialized mechanic who charges considerably more than a regular mechanic. The same is true for sports clubs, which usually differ only by name from the outside, but are radically different when it comes to philosophy or training methods.

How many have quit a sport or changed training groups because the training or competitive program of the former is not like "everybody else," or does not adhere to preconceived notions?

But, then, how many athletes doing the same training as all others have won world or Olympic championships?

For those of a more philosophical nature, the lessons contained herein can be applied to life itself. After all, do not the basics of every culture and religion, whether they be called laws, rules, or commandments, emphasize the control of one's basic instincts in order to show respect for others? Perhaps this is why the martial arts have long been associated with religious or mystical qualities. Figure skater Elvis Stojko, one of Glen Doyle's students in the martial arts, has an unprecedented record in terms of time and achievement at the top of the international competition ladder, even overcoming injury shortly before a major championship. Has he achieved success because of his overwhelming talent in a field laden with talent, or because of his longevity, his ability to avoid the "burn-out" that has afflicted many others? Elvis Stojko avoided burn-out with his ability to relax and focus, two aspects ingrained in the martial arts.

Glen Doyle would probably be the first to admit that those able to apply the more subtle teachings of the martial arts to themselves will be a minority in our "instant-gratification" society. But, in the words of poet Robert Frost,

"Two roads diverged in a wood, and I—
I took the one less traveled by,
And that has made all the difference."

Best Regards,
Bruce Burton, BSc, MPA

The following pages are not meant to be lawmakers, or lawbreakers with regard to the martial arts. They have been written to try to help guide those without fighting experiences, and perhaps somehow enlighten those who have it. Please try to look upon this book as an "old friend" you can turn to once in a while for sound advice or guidance.

Glen Doyle

INTRODUCTION

From the first moment we enter the world to our final days, we as human beings look to both order and chaos to balance themselves and allow threads of peace and contentment to taper our lives. However, many times we find that this balance is not so easily achieved and we look for other ways to find that elusive peace of mind. This is of course our natural desire to speed up the process. We don't want to have to wait twenty to thirty years for the balance to find us, so we go forth and try to muscle the balance into place.

What constitutes balance in an individual's life is a very personal and unique thing. What one person calls balance, another would call chaotic...and what another calls chaotic, one might call peaceful. The factors that influence this state of thinking depend on numerous variables that would be impossible to expand on in one simple book.

It should be evident to all that society as a whole is constantly changing. It is this constant change that allows trends, laws, and even philosphies to become "popular" or "old fashioned." This constant change can affect the simplest of inventions to the most intricate of thoughts, but, none the less, change takes place.

Ever-changing means ever-forward, and ever-forward means swift adaptation or extinction. With so many variables, how is anyone to comprehend what life is to be? Welcome, friends, welcome to the martial arts. For if a person is looking for an idea or thought that has a constant thread, no matter what time period they happen to grace, then one can turn to the martial arts world—the constant...the relentless...the balanced!

Within these pages you will find my thoughts, feelings, and theories of the fighting world. These ideas are based upon both experience and trial. Though no one can guarantee that you will agree or disagree with the following pages, it is hoped that this book will be able to offer something to every reader. If you are a novice in the arts (less than a year), this book can help you through the first few pivotal choices of your martial arts journey, from your first training routines to your personal view of the entire martial arts community. If you have just decided to take it up, I hope with this book to put you on your correct pathway before you start, from choosing a proper style, to actual competition and street use. For those of you who are already accomplished martial artists, I hope these pages will allow you to see what you have always known but chosen to ignore, or help to solidify your greatness within your art. Perhaps it will open that one fleeting element in your art that you have been unable to conquer.

Whatever the case, if from these pages you walk away with one new way of looking at the martial arts, my time and effort will have been worth it. My goal is not to impose my personal views upon you, but rather to get you to look into yourself for the true guidance that should govern all of the elements in your life.

Good luck!
Glen Doyle

Choosing a Style

In the bustle and bustle of a crazy day and age, the martial arts are becoming more and more popular as a means of escape from the day-to-day tortures of the community. People are beginning to look to the martial arts not only for physical fitness, but also as guidance to a stress-free existence. Unfortunately, up to half of all martial art practitioners may be studying the wrong style! This is not to say that the style they are studying holds no merit, but rather the practitioner is wasting valuable energy trying to mold their bodies to a form of combat that neither the mind nor the body feels comfortable doing.

Choosing a martial art is one of the most important things any one person can do in their respective lifetimes, not only because of the nature of the practice, but also because of the side effects of the practice. Anyone who has studied a martial art will tell you that the *art in question* never stays at the club or area of practice; sometime, sooner or later, the style will begin to find its way into every facet of your life. It is for this reason, and this reason alone, that a decision to study should not be made in haste.

The fact that a decision is even being made about martial art study should itself be scrutinized. When an individual makes the decision to study a warring art, the reason for this decision often escapes them. This in no way means that they should forget their martial art dreams, but they should look deep into themselves to be confident that the reason is a valid reason indeed—not a passing urge.

If one wishes to gain confidence, improve health and conditioning, or even immerse oneself in another culture, then one's martial art journey should be a long and fruitful one. However, if the only ideas that run through the mind are to "kick some butt" or to impress the "babes"—please…go bowling. A martial art is not just physical domination training, but, as all arts, much, much more.

Martial: Of or suitable for war or combat.

Art: Creative work or its principles; making or doing of things that display form, beauty, and unusual perception.

Putting these two definitions together should give a very good indication as to why many would-be masters fall into the depths of delinquency. This study is not something that is done once a week and then forgotten. Martial arts are life: they live, they breathe, they have their own personalities, and their own problems—they have heroes and villains, and the last thing they need is some "joker" trying to become a poor imitation of Bruce Lee or Chuck Norris in ten easy lessons.

When entering the martial arts, one must realize that there is an entirely new world to be discovered. It is because of this that only the mature, dedicated, and genuine student will excel. It is the seriousness of the study that will carry a new student through the (for lack of a better term) "infant" stage.

Because of its complexity, many new students feel that they are being led by the hand through their chosen martial art—and they are. It is at this time that the ego shows itself as enemy or ally, and from there it is up to the practitioner to take it wherever he or she wishes to take it.

Just deciding to take a martial art is a big step, but it is only one of many. Of all initial decisions, the one involving the style to study will be the biggest and most important.

A style will have specifics, distinct characteristics, manner of expressions, executions, and philosophies, and it is for these reasons that research into different styles is vital. The style you choose will become part of your everyday routine. It will reflect you, your club, and your instructor. Choosing an unsuitable or inappropriate form of combat to match with your personality and life-style will not only be a huge mistake, but could eliminate any chance of martial art prowess whatsoever.

When choosing a style one must take into account numerous external influences. The biggest mistake made by a new practitioner (or even by someone who has stuck it out in another style for years) is the lack of thought regarding your body. Your body is the main element of yourself that will be doing much of the work, so naturally you would want to pick something that would benefit your body rather than damage it. We all seem to be able to decide wisely when it only involves personal taste, ideas, or practicality, but when we throw ourselves into the physical realm (from jogging to weight lifting and everything in between) we discard our practical sense and look to aesthetics to make our decision. The best choice for an individual relies on the *absence of sale*. You decide on something based on research, knowledge, and common sense. To further illustrate this point, answer the following:

You live on a farm; it rains a lot, it snows a lot. You have to deliver your crops to the town market every second day. You decide to buy a vehicle to help you. What would you buy?

a)   a Ferrari

b)   a motorcyle

c) a mountain bike

d) a four-wheel-drive pick-up truck

Halfway through the above question the answer had already come to you. Why? Because it was the most obvious, and common sense prevailed in seconds. Why should your thought process be any different when it comes to your body and the way you work it? Here is the same question asked differently:

You're nineteen years old, 5'7" tall, 124 lb., dislike violence, never had a fight in your life, love Japanese culture. You would study:

a) Karate (power with power)

b) Boxing (blow for blow)

c) Thai boxing (crippling)

d) Kyudo (Japanese archery)

The same question asked yet again: You're twenty-seven years old, 6'2" tall, 200 lb., lift weights, work at a bar as a doorman (bouncer)—lots of agression. You would study:

a) Tai Chi (meditative)

b) Fencing (swordplay)

c) Tae Kwon Do (kicking)

d) Judo (art of grappling)

Although anyone could answer YES to any of the choices, realistically some would not be very logical. A bouncer studying fencing? It may improve his coordination and his reflexes, but when he "touches" some huge, violent drunk in a valiant attempt to get him out of the club, there could be trouble. Studying Judo, the doorman would not only increase his percentage of success at his job, he would probably learn to do it easier and with less threat of injury to both himself and his opponent.

Taking that first step is not an easy one, but don't make it harder by choosing something that will not suit you. When choosing a martial art, look at yourself: your size, weight, athletic history. Look at your personality. Are you aggressive? Do you avoid confrontation? Are you seeking a confidence builder?

There are literally thousands of questions you could ask, but only ask enough questions to get a fair idea of what you wish to accomplish. Once you know what you are basically looking for, do some research. Just as everything in fighting should have a purpose, so should decisions and the reasoning process leading to them. Don't leap into something that may require a total personality or mental overhaul. In the martial arts, change is part of the process. Choosing a style that closely resembles your life-style will not only speed up the learning process but will also enhance your already positive attributes.

While you are researching, you will more than likely find three or four styles that appeal to you, which is good, because you've already narrowed it down. You have chosen four styles from literally hundreds. Now you can continue your research on the select few. Find out everything there is to know about them: the type of people that study, the type of people that teach, and the general purpose of the style. Do they employ more kicks than punches? Do they punch or kick at all? Do they use weapons? Do they wrestle? Do they use force?

All the above questions should be answered and laid out in front of you. Once your research is complete, stop and look at what you've got. By the time you've done the research for the selected styles, perhaps two have piqued your interest. This is good. Again, the selection process is continuing. You will begin to notice similarities between the list of your own characteristics, and that of the styles you have selected. The selection process is becoming easier.

The reason for doing all of the above is to save time, energy, and money. Literally years of sweat and toil have been lost by individuals who later realized that they have chosen the wrong style and have robbed themselves of the chance to excel at a style that was more suitable for them.

The entrapment of the martial arts is a universal thing, and all styles have it. It is not done on purpose, nor is it readily known even by those instructing...it just happens.

Martial arts training is so vast and subjective that one's lack of connection with their chosen style can go unnoticed because of the philosophy "it takes time," "no one becomes great overnight," and "it requires sacrifice."

Though this philosophy holds true even if the proper style is chosen, the rewards are totally different. Realizing that a style may not be right for you after you have started your training may take months or years. Know what you're taking before you start, don't be bullied, impressed, or even begged. Fall back on your-self, because only you know what is right for you.

So many times we ignore that little voice inside us. When choosing a martial art, more times than not, that little voice is right. We all have built-in instincts that are geared to help us avoid bad situations or people. Why not call upon this gift to help choose an article of existence or improvement of existence like the fighting arts?

Although there is no checklist to help you decide, by look-ing at yourself and looking at the options, you will have a better than average chance of enjoying your martial arts journey. Enjoyment will lead to a longer learning curve and will keep the mind and body hungry for more.

Make all decisions with thought, research, and resource. By doing this, you will increase the chance of picking the style that will mold to your personality perfectly, and in this, your martial art journey will be long and full of knowledge.

C H A P T E R   T W O

Choosing a School

The battle for hearts and minds continues—theory versus experience, the old sage against the young upstart—the battle rages on. But no matter how the battle rages, all thought, whether tainted or assisted by life, must admit to one thing: school has its place. And because education is a process not a result, area of study is probably more important to martial art prowess than one would think.

Environment has always helped in the forming of personal opinions, ideals, and outlooks on life in general. We are what we see; we become what we wish to imitate; and we imitate what makes us comfortable. Because of this, it would only follow that something as familiar to us as our home town reputation or image will filter its way into our own personality. So too for martial art institutions.

To try to describe a martial arts school is a near impossibility. This is a place that not only helps create an individual, but also reflects both the teacher and style in question. It can create greatness or can instill in an individual attitudes and beliefs that are both self-serving and bigoted. A school is a place of learning...learning is growth...growth is evolution.

A school, club, or dojo is the area in which martial art styles house their very identities. There is a distinct difference between training in some barn or garage and training in a "temple-like" palace, but of the two, is there any difference in the caliber of teaching? The answer is not really. If a teacher can teach you a perfect punch in his multimillion dollar franchised school, then odds are that he can do the same in an old, run-down garage. Granted, it may be a little more uncomfortable, but the style should not suffer. Just because a person decides to train in a garage, doesn't mean the style they teach is trash. It does state, however, something about the individual running the club.

A martial art school does *not* have a physical appearance formula; there is no right or wrong. What makes a school great is its teachers and its product. Would you judge a chef by his kitchen or by the taste of his food? In all fairness, some people may indeed look to the kitchen for some guidance, but the basis for any decision would be the actual enjoyment of the food.

Therefore, choosing a school must be done as carefully as choosing a style: both must fit an individual like a glove.

In this world of frauds and scam artists, one cannot be too careful when deciding to choose a school. Because not only could this be an expensive mistake, it also could be both physically and mentally damaging. Remember, you are about to put all this new-found knowledge into your mind, thoughts, and physical state. If the school is not genuinely interested in you, then all your time and energy will not only be wasted, but it may take you years to filter out the terrible things you have learned—which unfortunately might lead you to be disillusioned when you might have otherwise been a great complement to the art.

Your chosen school will be your home away from home, and because of this fact it must be a good one. Characteristics of a school will be evident by the type of students the school turns out. A school that has little or no genuine contact with the practitioner will generally create self-centered students with attitudes that are both self-serving and uncontrollable.

In any good school there is what is known as a *pecking order*, a *system of ranking*. This system is not in place to belitttle or abuse, but rather to keep everything in order, respectful. This is one area in which a lot of schools find problems. Ranking, though needed, gives an illusion of a beginning and an end. In the Japanese styles everybody is looking for the black belt. The Korean and some hybrid Chinese schools follow the same program. If you learn just one thing from this entire book, let it be this: martial art study has *no beginning* and it has *no end*. It is continuous until the day we leave this world. Achieving black belts in a chosen style should only indicate the new journey for personal knowledge and technical fulfillment. Be like a circle: continuous, ever-forward, improvisational.

To choose a school, one must, again, do research—but this time the research comes in the form of observation. All that is basically required is energy and time expended to travel to different areas to see what each school teaching your chosen art has to offer.

In most schools, there is an allotted time for visitors. It is during this time that you, as the interested party, should begin to make mental notes of your visit. The notes should encompass not only the personality of the club, but the students, the instructor, and the attitude toward you as a visitor.

Many times what schools like to do is set up a private interview where you talk one-on-one with the head instructor-owner (whatever). What this does is give you a sense of importance. Also it gives the interviewer the opportunity to force an answer out of you right away. Many people feel guilty when someone has given up their time for them. **Don't fall into this trap**.

Another drawback to the one-on-one interview is simply lack of evidence. You, as the interested party, have no chance to view the talent of both the school and the instructor. If you're going to put your money down (not to mention your physical availability), you should at least have some knowledge of your potential instructor's prowess. Always remember: **see what you're buying**.

Another thing to watch for is the invisible Grandmaster—this mystic teacher (usually the founder of the club) who never seems available to teach. Many of the not-so-honest schools create these mysterious masters in hopes of persuading innocents to join the establishment and learn secret techniques and styles. When dealing with school research, **believe nothing that you hear, and only half of what you see**.

Everyone wants to believe the seemingly impossible: the *Dim Mak* master who can kill you by touching you, the Shaolin monk who can levitate his entire body, the Chi Kung master who can throw you across the room, yet never lay a finger on you, and my personal favorite, "this guy taught Bruce Lee."

It is a given that the martial arts are as old as time itself. We agree that the physical attributes of men and women 700 years ago would have been different from now, but jumping over a house? Yet, every day there are schools feeding this crap into new, wide-eyed hopefuls with dreams of grandeur. Understand this: no one is untouchable, and no one is unbeatable, though they can help teach you methods to lower the percentage of strikes reaching you, or protect to the point of saving lives. **Come to terms with this thought: if you fight, you're gonna get hit!**

Next, "The Champion Schools"—usually a club or academy that has been started by a former tournament or fighting great. These schools ride the wave of the owner's success and try to attract students through the promise of association. Now, someone who has won tournaments or fighting matches has definitely put in their time, but before you sign on the dotted line, **be sure they can pass on their knowledge**.

I've met many a champion (some undefeated in their style) who have zero ability to teach. I'm not trying to take away from their reputations, but they had no clue how to pass on their skill. The style worked for them, and they proved themselves to be great, but it won't guarantee that they'll be great teachers. Teaching is a gift, plain and simple, and though a fighting great may have had the gift for combat, the teaching arena is a totally new game.

Champion clubs are an outstanding decision if the champion can pass on the skill. Again, before you put your money down, watch some classes and see how he or she instructs, or if they even instruct at all.

Finally, we get the most notorious of offenders: the "Hollywood Schools." This basically entails a club trying to promote themselves as the all-style school, to try and snare those impressed by movie greats like Bruce Lee, Chuck Norris, and so on. Many times you'll see a school advertise something like: John Doe's Martial Arts Academy (karate, kung-fu, jiu jitsu, kickboxing, tai chi, and whatever style is popular at the time). I've even come across a bogus club advertising that they not only taught Chinese *kung-fu*, but Chinese *gung-fu* as well (they are *exactly* the same thing!).

Always remember, it takes years to become truly proficient in a given style. Anyone who claims mastery of numerous styles is really pushing it. Actually, anyone who claims mastery in one style is really pushing it. My sifu always told me: "For someone to call themselves a Master, martial arts is the only thing they do. They sleep, eat, and drink only martial arts—that is what they are—it is all they are." If they have interests, jobs, or responsibilities outside the club, then they better stick with the more reserved sifu or sensei title.

There is one aspect of the martial arts world that has changed the face of both teaching quality and student dedication or loyalty to a school or club: business, the nature of the beast.

Fighting is an art and takes years to learn and hopefully perfect, and nothing looks as incredible as a perfectly executed technique. It won't come cheap, but this is not to say that higher costs means a better school or style.

Martial arts is a business like any other; they need your money to survive. How do you get money? Advertising, marketing, specials, deals, promises, and so on. Do not get caught up in the hype—the martial art scam artists can see you coming a mile away, and because the martial arts are something that take years to learn, you may not be able to realize the rip-off for a number of months, or even years. If you go to a school named after the owner and you are going to pay money, then you had better be trained by the owner and not some hot-shot fancy pants that can fake it better than the "mystic owner" himself. You paid for quality; make sure you get it.

Business is business, but art is time-consuming, and time is money; watch out for this vicious circle. Beware of long contracts that require yearly memberships or clubs that make you pay for everything (uniform, tests, forms, etc). Granted, a lot of times these extra charges are needed to help maintain the club, but don't let them get out of hand. Look for a school where respect for the instructor leads to respect for other students, but more importantly, leads to respect for yourself.

In the vast world of the martial arts there are both saints and sinners. Take your time, look at all your options. Find a place that allows you to learn at a comfortable pace, where you are allowed to grow as an individual—a place that you would be proud to call home.

No one should learn through intimidation. You should learn through proper teaching technique and dedication. If a school tries to push itself upon you, whether by big promises or intimidation, realize one thing—that is most likely how they teach their style.

A style and school will mold you into the new, improved person that you wish to become, a person that was always there but has decided to ascend to higher levels. Don't sell yourself short. Set your expectations high so that both the style and school you choose will hopefully be quality based to fit your every need. When we have choices in food, clothing, and luxuries, we never sell ourselves short. Why now? If a doctor was about to give you a vaccination and had two needles ready, and he tells you that the yellow needle is a proven cure and it is perfect to battle your infection…and then tells you that the green needle may cure what you have but there are no guarantees—which vaccination are you going to take?

Be selfish, be inwardly egotistical—get the best for you and you alone. Look for nothing but the best. You are about to inject this martial art knowledge into your mind, your body, every facet of your life…make sure that both the cure (style) and the doctor (instructor) are the best…for you.

CHAPTER THREE

Making Your Style "Yours"

When we are given something, whether it be by choice or by surprise, we as human beings immediately decide if it is for us, meaning, will it fit our way of thinking, our style? We will always try to change and mold things to more readily complement our persona; the martial arts should be no different. When an individual buys a creative product (such as paints, wallpaper, etc.) the idea behind this is to add a personal touch. The satisfaction a person feels when he (or she) enters an area that he has helped create cannot be measured. Why do people take pride in their homes? Why do some people decide to make their own clothing? It all comes down to personal satisfaction and identity.

When this lesson filters its way into the life of the martial artist, not only do identity and satisfaction become magnified, but something else begins to surface: a better martial artist, with cleaner techniques, faster reaction times, and an overall ability to fuse his or her martial arts training into every facet of day-to-day living.

As with many things in life, the martial arts strive for that ever-changing element, something to avoid the perils of complacency and completion.

As I have said, your martial arts study should be a circle— having no beginning and no end. A person should never see an end to the learning process, no matter what age or how much time was spent training.

Throughout the total learning process (which may span decades), as discussed in Chapter 7, a martial artist will encounter times of seemingly fruitless training, time spent when no one really feels that they have improved—the plateau.

A practitioner will experience many of these while learning a chosen style. They should not be avoided, they cannot be avoided, and if anything, they are an indication of the progress you've already made. Reaching a plateau means you have ascended from your earlier talents—and plateaus have a secret benefit that few realize.

When a person becomes proficient in a chosen martial art and they find that their learning curve or progression is unacceptably slow, they seem to do one of two things. Either they turn inward and become displeased with themselves—their genetics, their entire physical being—or they begin to look at their style as incomplete or lacking for their needs. Don't get discouraged!

It must be understood that although physical attributes will tend to determine a person's speed in learning a skill, it does not dictate the learning style. What this means is simply that the beauty of the martial arts is the ability to turn weaknesses into strengths. A physical disadvantage becomes the point of origin for the attributes one will eventually possess.

Now, when dealing with incomplete styles, this gets a little tricky. *It must be admitted that every style has at least one inherited weakness, something not as prominent as in other styles.* For instance, certain styles of Hung Gar kung-fu lack skills of ground fighting techniques, but there are few styles existing that can match its raw power (pound for pound). All a Hung Gar practitioner need do is train from strength. Rather than abandon the punching power of Hung Gar and jump to a grappling art, the practitioner should incorporate some grappling basics into his punching techniques. In this way the style becomes stronger, as does the practitioner.

When an individual reaches a plateau, it is time to begin to change the body's *circuitry*. Circuitry is the way the mind deciphers information and calculates the proper response. In reality, anyone who studies a martial art is doing this in some way by trying to learn things to override fear, increase confidence, or simply maintain a healthy frame of mind.

When we discuss making your style "yours," it means to take what you have learned and recircuit yourself to make it work that much better. Do not mistake recircuiting for changing your style. All that is to be done is to take the techniques from your chosen martial art and use them to fit your qualifications.

Example: Three people learn to throw an uppercut
(aimed under the opponent's chin).
Person A: Male, 280lb., 6'2" tall, 23 years old.
Person B: Female, 105lb., 5'2" tall, 45 years old.
Person C: Male, 118 lb., 5'0" tall, 58 years old.

Now looking at the list above, and given that they all learn the same style, started at the same time, and have only had this martial art training as experience...do you really think they will all throw the uppercut in the exact same manner?

The answer should be NO! We are not even taking into account the situation that they might be using the uppercut in, we're just using their physical attributes as evidence.

Though there are hundreds of possible answers, we should just try to come up with a few. It should be obvious to all that *Person A* would easily be allowed to rely on sheer physical strength, whereas *Person B* and *Person C* may have to incorporate twisting or hip movements to accelerate the technique or increase power: That is circuitry.

Saying this, fighters should use the plateaus they encounter in practices as time to discover themselves. Only by knowing your own strengths and weaknesses can you ever hope to accelerate your learning. Think of it...you reach a plateau and you can't seem to improve. You step out of yourself and begin to analyze all things about you. Suddenly you realize that one of your kicks can be done a certain way because of your natural flexibility. Or because of that old shoulder injury, your backfist techniques should rely more on speed than power...are you southpaw or orthodox? So many times a person will try a technique or exercise and take it gift-wrapped and never look inside, but to truly appreciate the gift, one has to open the present and look at it from all angles.

What Helps to Make Your Style Yours?

Take Into Account Your Body Type

Body size will make the difference in individuality. A large, burly practitioner will rely more on power than speed, whereas a small person will incorporate speed, finesse, and muscle explosion to create his or her own rhythm.

Take Into Account Your Personality

A person's way of acting or reacting will influence style. If you are quiet and introverted then you may become what is called a reactionary—your style will rely upon the attacker always making the first move...in this your personality will be both useful and instinctive to help launch counterattacks and defenses. If you are aggressive and confident, then more likely your fighting persona would be that of a hunter. You'll initiate more during combat—exploding in movement and first strikes.

Take Into Account Your Preferred Appendage

Do you prefer kicking or hand techniques? Recircuiting should match the mind; do not fight it. Comfort will be the ultimate quest. A major mistake that many martial artists make when they fight is the abandonment of their chosen style. So many times a puncher will ignore his or her strength and get into a wrestling match with the opponent...all this tells me is that the puncher has either not recircuited properly or he or she has studied the wrong style. Know yourself...sooner or later your style will know itself within you.

Take Into Account Your Style's Strength

Knowing your style's strong point helps both you and the style. First, when recircuiting, the style's strength will be magnified once it has adhered to your individuality. Secondly, you will make both your style and your teacher look impressive. It's now through you that both the style and the teachers of this style are reflected. If your style has great kicks, then leg and hip explosion will probaby be the initial recircuiting area. Punching styles will incorporate more explosion from the hip and shoulder, and grappling styles will incorporate more spine and neck manipulation.

To look too much into recircuiting could also be dangerous. Recircuiting is, simply stated, changing your mind's set rhythms to that of your fighting style so that both can work together and at the same time operate independently. In this, your enemies can never get set against you. Your ability to switch from *contemporary* back to *classical* to your *recircuited version* gives you three styles in one.

Although there is no checklist to tell someone if they have successfully recircuited themselves, there are some guidelines you may want to follow:

1. **Start with the basic techniques of your style.**
   By starting with the basics, you will begin to get a good understanding of yourself, something that you can use as text when you start to recircuit the more intricate techniques.

2. **If it doesn't "feel" right it's probably wrong.**
   Your body is your best teacher—it has guided you since birth—so don't ignore its messages. If while trying to recircuit you feel uncomfortable, awkward, pain, off-balance, and so on, then your mind (which knows you better than anyone) is telling you to keep adjusting: you don't quite have it.

3. **Subconscious guidelines are the best.**
   When you learn a martial art, there will be one or two techniques that will already be perfectly suited to

27

you. You will find that certain techniques are so natural that you don't have to think about them…they just happen. These are the techniques that are already circuited and they can be great guidelines. Once you realize your "subconscious" techniques, use them. Perform them and get to know that feeling of comfort so that when you are recircuiting the other techniques, you know the feeling you're looking for.

4. **Never model yourself after someone else.**
   This should be self-explanatory. You are an individual: You are not your teacher, you are not your partner, you are not your friend. You are you…and that should be your creator.

5. **Always keep your classical foundations.**
   When making your style yours, do not abandon your background. This means don't condemn or ridicule the classical styles you have been taught—they are invaluable. Though it may be true that once you have recircuited yourself and your style of martial art is totally yours, remember where your style came from—CLASSICAL MARTIAL ARTS. Without classical foundations none of your circuiting would have been possible, and it is the classical techniques that have allowed you to improve yourself to the point of recircuiting.

Recircuiting may take both practice and patience, but the by-product is invaluable. Once an individual has successfully recircuited themselves, he or she has not only improved fighting prowess, but is ready to return to classical study with that much more insight. Stepping outside yourself is a difficult thing to do. It requires the ability to see yourself as flawed. Ego will many times stand in the way of a martial artist's ability. But remember, if you are to bring honor to your chosen style and maybe even add something to it for future generations, then be ready and willing to inject a little of yourself into your martial art. Help mold its future.

Psychological Makeup

As an individual learns and grows, external factors affect thoughts, feelings, and preferences. A young child may hate the six o'clock news, thinking it a waste of time and not fun at all. However, as that child lives and grows both physically and mentally, and as his mind is bombarded by new ideas and thought patterns, the now young adult not only begins to like the six o'clock news, but perhaps actually starts to look forward to it.

New discoveries and tasks lead you to reassess what you have been taught, or allows you to conceive entirely new ideals that will govern your thoughts and actions until they are again changed. Outside influences can come in many forms: new friends, a new job with new job skills, education, and, of course, the martial arts. Any and all things can redirect your initial ideals and principles, but you must always keep in mind that change is a two-headed coin, and you must take the good with the bad.

As in any decision in life, there will be influences that will change your attitude. Whether these changes come in the physical or mental form, they nevertheless do exist.

Because the study of the martial arts incorporates the mind, body, and spirit, it should be common sense that directs the eventual change in attitude, thought patterns, and maybe even dress or musculature. However, the greatest change that can have both positive and negative results on the practitioner is that of demeanor.

When someone enters the training realm, they are there to learn, advance, and grow. The whole process of training is purely for skill and personal advancement, but what people don't take into account is the other changes that will occur.

Because no two people are identical, personality changes or consistencies will vary from person to person. It has been my experience that there are usually three general personality changes that an individual who chooses the martial art pathway will experience. These changes are gradual and may take a number of years to run the cycle, but they are part of every style and discipline.

Do not try and avoid these changes because they are part of the martial art rule. These changes are needed to help you grow in your newfound fighting arts realm. The changes should be monitored and (if possible) regulated so as not to take away from the art that you are learning, but in no way should you alter the course you have chosen.

Though there will be many students of martial arts who will deny a personality change in either themselves or anyone they know who studies, for your convenience I have broken down the general personality changes into the three simplest stages. Though the stages may vary in intensity and length, they will be present and somewhat noticeable. These stages are usually the periods when an instructor gets a rather good idea what he or she is dealing with.

Stage 1: The Know-It-All

When students first enter their chosen school, they are more times than not humble and eager to listen. They are eager because of the hunger for advancement, and this hunger will get them to concentrate and push themselves farther than normal.

In the first year, practitioners will see the greatest increase in their martial art skill. This is basically due to the lack of skill they had when they began. Their mind starts to comprehend more, and their bodies do the same. Things that just a few months ago seemed impossible for them to achieve are now easily within their grasp.

There is nothing more pleasurable to a teacher or a student than to see great change—but great change requires great responsibility.

Unfortunately, when a lot of new students begin to learn at what *they* perceive as an accelerated rate, their thoughts about themselves also start to change. Phrases like "I'm gifted," "I'm so natural at this," "I can't believe I learned this already," begin to race through each of their minds.

Keep in mind that a student should not be blamed for these thoughts. They should be guided even more, because the basic reason for thinking they are the next Bruce Lee is probably due to the shallow goals they created for themselves in the first place.

Again, going back to their very first day at the club, they see individuals doing things that look magical. And now a few months later, they are beginning to do the very same things they once held in reverence. Wouldn't you feel god-like?

The danger is not in the thoughts the students have about themselves, but rather in the way the rest of the outside world sees them. The know-it-all attitude has gotten more martial artists into trouble than any other. The way a person walks becomes a strut, their talk becomes challenging, and their thoughts are tainted with arrogance and false confidence.

In this stage, anything these students see as an attempt at martial arts outside their club will be challenged. A student in this stage looks upon all other martial arts and artists as inferior. If he sees two people play-fighting or throwing kicks at each other, the practitioner seems to take this as a challenge. The two people may have never seen him before, but may have to put up with snide remarks or even a verbal challenge. It's all part of the know-it-all frame of mind.

With respect to the individual, each practitioner will go through this stage at a different level. Some may be very noticeable whereas others may slip your attention. But whatever the case, keep in mind the growth potential of the individual and keep in mind your own growth. If these growing spurts were not to take place, then the martial arts would have died off centuries ago.

Stage 2: The Passive Monk

One thing that movies and the media are responsible for is the enigmatic martial arts personality. How many times have you watched a film about the quiet, peaceful martial artist who takes as much as he or she can until they snap? This stereotypical persona has filtered its way into every facet of the real-life martial arts realm. Because of this, it should not come as a surprise that this way of thinking will in one way or another affect the attitudes of a real-life practitioner. Welcome to the second stage of a fighter's mental progression.

This manner of thinking usually follows after stage 1. Opposites usually compliment each other, so for as much as the first stage boasts egocentricity, the second stage boasts an over-abundance of humility.

This is not to say that this stage is not a welcome change from the previous, but that this personality is not realistic. Society has changed so much throughout the ages that this type of thinking is not safe. Granted that a humble person is nice to be around, and granted that any true martial artist does not outwardly brag about the skill they possess. There is, however, a difference between humility and victimization. Turning the other cheek is not wrong, but in certain situations it can be dangerous. Given the situation, one must look for an answer in the events to come, but if the practitioner is too set on avoiding trouble by taking the "Shaolin monk" approach, then they are potentially putting themselves at risk.

The bad element of today (the average street fighter) will not look upon your patience and nonviolent attitude as honorable (like in the movies), rather, he will look upon it as weakness. Though this attitude can be applied in degree to a number of situations, the streets of today are too harsh.

No one will look upon the passive martial artist as a person set in his or her ways, but rather as someone who has little or no faith in a chosen style.

Remember, avoiding violence is preferable, but don't become a victim because of a melodramatic "Saturday action theatre" movie that was set in the 15th century. Live in the present and always be prepared.

Stage 3: The Echo

The first two stages both have one redeeming quality: they supply knowledge to the third stage. More specifically, the first two become entwined to form the hybrid stage known as "The Echo."

This is basically the third and final stage of martial art personality development. The attitude here is one of a mature, confident (but not arrogant) fighter who will fight when it is unavoidable and will walk away smiling when the antagonists are not worth the bother. Again, there is no set time frame to reach this level. For some it may come in a few years and for others a little longer. If your school is good, your instructor caring and wise, and your fellow students supportive, then your journey to this stage will be a little smoother.

The benefits of this stage are really immeasurable. Usually after reaching this stage the practitioner will be assigned teaching duties. The practitioner will begin to look deeply at his or her chosen art (as well as the arts of others) for good and bad qualities. It is believed that no single style is perfect. Every style has an inborn weakness, something that can be improved on. It is only by being mentally mature that a practitioner can begin to dissect his style in the search for the ultimate cure to make the style complete.

During this stage, one may begin to think about other styles, incorporating other strong-points with those of his own style. Perhaps the strength of one style can complement the weaknesses of another. In this, the practitioner begins to view all things as useful, yet it allows him to ignore those that are of no personal use (with regards to size, strength, and personal fighting nature).

Be prepared for changes, but don't try to fight them. Rather, understand them, listen to what they tell you, and try to get as much out of them as possible...for you, your style, your school.

CHAPTER FIVE

The Street

The street is the territory in which deeds, not words, speak volumes. It is the uncontrollable domain, where fighting prowess is not gauged by the beauty of the technique, but rather by its efficiency in destroying an enemy—this is the street.

This ever-changing realm of violence has always tested the martial artist. Moments can decide the course of a lifetime, and emotions can make or break a victory. The street is where ranking means little, and actions must be backed with nerve, accuracy, and bone-crushing power.

When trying to find the true essence of who he is, a person will sometimes go back and trace his roots: where he came from and what were the attitudes and ideals that made his people or culture distinct. This allows him to create for himself a sense of identity, but more so, to create guidelines for achieving a desired result (i.e., a person of Irish descent born in Canada may frequent Irish pubs with an "Irish" crowd, in the hopes that some "Irishness" may rub off.)

Basically, everything in life has a background, roots, and things developed from situational reactions. So when dealing with the trials and tribulations of the street, the martial arts has a good history.

For the longest time, the "street problem" has been a dark cloud for the martial artist. A technique, no matter how well it looks or works in the club, seems to be questioned—will it work in the street?

What one must remember is that the street is an uncontrolled element. It has more variables than any other area in the martial art world. But to question a martial art technique is, in reality, very insulting.

Everyone may agree that because of the danger of modern day streets, people will naturally question technique. However, if you look back at the art's origin, some solace may be found.

The martial arts are warring techniques—movements used to kill—period. Because of this finality, the martial arts have had the best evolutionary process of anything in history. Think of it, if a thousand years ago a martial arts master used a technique that was useless, chances are he or she was killed while using that technique. With that master dead, that "inferior" technique would not be taught, not passed on. On the other side of the coin, if a master had techniques that were so accurate and proficient that he defeated all of his foes, the master lived to teach these techniques, and the chances of the students continuing to use these techniques increased, as did the probability of passing the knowledge on to their students.

You have at your fingertips an art that has gone through about 2000 years of evolution. Think of it, 2000 years of weeding out useless techniques—in fact, up until the last century, when the martial arts were no longer used so much for combat (weapons were becoming more advanced)—you had a pure combat style used for survival...period.

Now let's look to the modern day streets—not so scary, now, are they? The one thing a person must possess if he is to conquer that concrete jungle is confidence in his chosen style. If you don't believe that your style can protect you in the street, then stay home! The street has no allies, no areas of certainty. It's you against them, and everything is conquerable. Everything!

There are four golden rules about the street:

1. Be confident
2. Be smart
3. Be ready
4. If you can't take a punch, don't fight

Be Confident

Just as the saying "you are what you eat" guides a nutrition-conscious person, "walk like a victim" should indicate the outcome of the street scenario. The biggest problem with the street today is the victims themselves. When we talk about victims, this does not just mean those who have been beaten or robbed, but also those who are trapped at home for fear of the outside—such as martial artists fearing that their style will not work or worried that they might get hit, thus destroying the "magic image" of the martial arts.

When you walk, walk with a purpose. This does not guarantee that you will not be bothered, but it will more than likely make a would-be attacker think twice, which may be all you'll need. An attacker would much rather pursue a victim he knows he can intimidate easily rather than have to force the intimidation on you or work to frighten you.

Another by-product of confidence is clear thinking. This is invaluable to someone in a potentially dangerous situation. Clear thinking does something that many may not realize—it creates simplicity. When a person is attacked, the basic "flight or fight" reaction is initiated. However, if the fight instinct surfaces, that's only half the battle. What a practitioner must learn to avoid is *overload*. Simply stated, overload is the result of too many messages racing to the brain at the same time. The person is being attacked and because of panic, tries to recall every martial art technique he ever learned all at once. The result—an immobile victim.

However, if you have learned to harness your confidence, the thought process is clear and, more importantly, simple. The simple techniques will be the ones that save you. Simple, direct, to the point. What are simple techniques? Those techniques inside your subconscious, the techniques that have no thought process, just reaction and instinct.

This is why you should research yourself before you go venturing out on the street. Knowing yourself is as important as any technique ever taught. When you know yourself it not only increases your martial arts ability, but it allows for faster assessment.

If you know yourself, this means you understand thought processes, body language, action, and reaction. Granted that no one is the same, and it is almost guaranteed that the attacker will have a totally different way of thinking. However, because you, the martial artist, have this insight into living, breathing, and thinking, your chances of thwarting the attacker will be greater because of your control of the ever-changing variables. The ordinary thought process leads to complacency, whereas a "street sense" leads to reaction and instinct. When reaction and instinct begin to control your moves, thoughts, and attitudes, the chances for street survival is increased. Thoughts and ideas are always welcome, but at the appropriate times. If you're standing in front of a mugger pointing a knife at you, it's instinct time! When we don't have to think about technique because it flows from us naturally, it seems to push up our confidence level tenfold. This type of confidence cannot be taught to you. Develop it on your own, because it's your life on the line.

Be Smart

Smart may mean many things to many people, but on the street it means the difference between getting home or perhaps getting a one-way ticket to the morgue.

Smart thinking is more instinctive than some people want to believe. Do I get into the elevator with this stranger? Do I park my car here? Should I walk home alone? Should I lock my car door at this stop sign? Anyone would agree that the answers would depend on the feeling or instinct. Unfortunately, sometimes politeness, convenience, or denial override that instinctual thought process. People get into the elevator because they don't want to insult the person; parking the car here is closer to the destination; I've walked home a million times alone; no one is going to bother me at an intersection!

Being smart means simply to look out for yourself, take nothing for granted, and listen to that little voice telling you to stay away from that person!

Assess everything before acting. You may have parked your car in a very busy parking lot, but that was two o'clock in the afternoon, and you'll be working until nine o'clock tonight, and it'll be dark by then. You've walked home alone before, but this time your hands are full, or this time it's raining and you have a hood on, and can't see very well...and so on.

Deduce and plan...ALWAYS!

Be Ready

As any good martial arts teacher will tell you, anyone can win a fight if given the right circumstances. An individual who is unprepared or ignorant is a good example of how to never win or avoid a confrontation. No day is set in stone, anything can happen, and it could happen to you. This is not to say that you should walk around paranoid, but at least be aware of everything that could possibly affect your street interactions. Being ready leaves little to chance, and when dealing with street combat, chance can be deadly.

The streets of any city or town can be filled with beauty and wonder, gifts, surprises, and culture. They can house artifacts of science, history, and community spirit: things that make urban living enjoyable. However, always remember that the street can turn into a Pandora's box of evil and danger, and preparing and calling upon your faith in both yourself and your chosen style of combat could make all the difference in your life...and in saving it.

If You Can't Take A Punch, Don't Fight

Reading this rule has always made people frown. It may sound silly, but you must remember that no one is untouchable, and it only takes one good punch to end a fight. Realize that you're going to get hit if you fight—so make sure that you're going to last, at least through the first few punches.

Inability to take a hit is probably the deciding factor in street fight losses and victories. How will you know if you can take a hit? Trust me...if you study, listen, learn, and practice...you'll know.

The street is a challenge. Even if you don't consider yourself a "street person," think about this—we spend on average three years of our lives in front of street and traffic lights; we have to travel from work to home, from home to work, from home to visit family and friends, from home to the movies and theaters, from home to the supermarket, from work to restaurants, from restaurants to the bank, and so on. Getting from point A to point B is seemingly harmless, but remember, the conduit that allows you to travel between these two points are the *streets of your city or town*. So, with this in mind, we all need to consider ourselves as "street people" in one form or another. And, because we spend so much of our time in public areas, we had better control both sides of the equation. If not, you may just want to write a draft of your will now and avoid the rush.

If you're afraid of something, keep doing it until the fear goes away. The streets belong to all of us, so take your piece now, before both *you* and *it* get eaten alive.

The Killer Instinct

One of nature's most prized possessions is the thought process. This process is not segregated merely into conscious and unconscious mental activity, but also includes those feelings and characteristics that are inbred.

As we continue to evolve, our feelings about life, love, hope and even faith are in some small way governed by our instincts. It is instinct that becomes the father and mother of existence and the guide to progress and perfection.

Within the martial arts, instinct plays a major role. It can mean the difference between victory and defeat, and it can allow a coward to become a hero, or a hero to become a poltroon. No matter what the interpretation, the killer instinct has become the most misunderstood and misused element of the fighting world.

An enigmatic element of all fighting arts, this fearsome weapon has always been sought by martial arts practitioners. It not only demands respect from those challenged but also from those who possess it. Unfortunately, though, it gets little respect. Students and instructors alike make the same mistakes when dealing with this deadly predisposition. So many times instructors will use the term "killer instinct" to indicate the follow-through of a technique, or students will fool themselves into believing they possess it because of a fluid technique. But practitioners and instructors should understand that the killer instinct is an area of the mind that cannot be exercised, it cannot be "whipped into shape," and it cannot be subdued or even ignored. People must first realize that the killer instinct (for lack of a better description) is a living, breathing energy that sees no barriers and no limits. It is *not* needed, however, to practice the martial arts, but rather it is needed to achieve an indominitable fighting spirit and to release the ferocity and strength needed to get the job done.

Simply stated, you do not need the instinct to be a martial artist. The killer instinct only becomes a factor in true combat—in uncontrolled situations when analytical thought takes far too long.

What makes the killer instinct such a dangerous reality is its "constant" characteristic. Simply stated, the killer instinct cannot be turned off. It is there lurking in the background of the practitioner's mind, ready to propel the practitioner into the most dangerous of situations.

One aspect of the killer instinct that few people seem to realize is its origin. Despite what some people might try to tell you, the killer instinct cannot be trained or taught. It must already be there—you must be born with it. Many people go out of their way to try and harness this incredible power, but, if it isn't there, it never will be.

Mixing the killer instinct with your martial arts training is something that should be done slowly and with extreme care. Both the martial arts and the killer instinct itself have distinct characteristics (some of which may not fuse).

Basically, the *killer instinct is the readiness to finish off your opponent—no matter the circumstances, conditions, or thoughts of others around you.* A lot of martial artists (especially boxers), can call upon this instinct to get them through times deemed by others as unfavorable. In some ways, the killer instinct can be compared to the *chi* (inner strength). In times of need, the instinct can give the practitioner that extra push to go all the way. Like the chi, the instinct focuses the mind and body as one to finish the task that has been undertaken.

When the killer instinct kicks in, it initiates the "ever-forward" impetus. Whatever has confronted the individual will now be dealt with, no matter what the consequences to the body. What you as a martial artist must do is try to have some degree of control over your killer instinct.

Begin with the swallowing of the "rage" (which more often than not leads to the unleashing of the instinct). This in no way means that you should stifle your emotions. Anger, fear, and so on can be used to your benefit, and knowledge of rage allows you to let out bursts of instinct at strategic times.

By-products of the Emotions

So many times in the martial arts you will hear the teacher, sifu, or sensei talk about the emotionless fighter. This idea of the pure martial artist who does not react to anything with emotion is, in my opinion, smothering the style.

We are living, breathing creatures, so, taking away the elements of our mind that allow for individualization, lengthening, and maturing of our learning curves is ridiculous.

Without emotions, we would all be the same—robotic drones with no individualistic thought or opinions. Now don't mark me as a martial artist who doesn't believe in emotional control. I do. But I believe that our lives and martial arts can only benefit from the use of emotions in the proper way.

Instead of burying the emotions, we should use their by-products to strengthen every apect of our lives. By "byproducts," I mean that each emotion emits another quality in both our mind and body.

For simplicity's sake, I have narrowed the list down to the five basic emotions. Beside these emotions, I have listed the byproduct, which when used with your martial arts training or everyday living is not only beneficial, it's idealistic.

Five Emotions and Their Byproducts

Anger: Gives strength and bravery

Fear: Gives perception and insight

Love: Gives drive and desire

Sadness: Gives open-mindedness and acceptance

Happiness: Gives endurance

To go over the list briefly:

Anger

Anger is very self-evident. Anyone who has been angry feels the strength in their voice and fists. But the key is to harness that strength, to use it to your advantage rather than wasting it in a useless fit.

Fear

When in combat, having a sense of fear tunes up all your other senses. Because of your desire to avoid being struck or kicked, the mind increases each sense's awareness. It's when you give in to fear that you end up freezing or losing control.

Love

Love is perhaps the most powerful of our emotions. It can create or destroy an individual. The desire and drive that it gives to a human being can never be measured but, if harnessed properly, the byproducts of love can turn every moment in your chosen field into one filled with discovery and satisfaction.

Sadness

So many times looked upon as a negative or undesirable emotion, sadness is sometimes the most immediately beneficial of the five emotions. In a normal state of mind, we can house stubborn opposition to new ideas and thoughts. But when the mind is clouded with sad and melancholy thoughts, it looks to any and all external entities to direct the sadness away. We are more open to suggestions on how to deal with our problems, we sometimes find friendship in places we refused to look before, and we can become more talkative and outgoing to those we would normally avoid. Within martial arts, this emotion could get an individual to look at a technique, situation, or even a style in an entirely different light, and different approaches mean more options.

Happiness

Happiness is the most straightforward of the five emotions. Happiness gives endurance for the simple fact that you wish for the feeling to continue. Any activity that makes you feel this way can and will be performed for as long as you are physically able.

Again, with all the variables in life, the above is a brief and makeshift list. But it should be detailed enough to give you an idea of "emotional usage" rather than smothering. Use the byproducts to their fullest extent—keep them controlled to a degree—but discover yourself within their presence.

Applying this knowledge to the killer instinct, we can now reiterate the need for its reality, as well as your ability to gauge both its power and strength. For as much as it is your ally, should you let it get the better of you, it will become an enemy.

For instance, if boxers didn't have the incredible control over their killer instinct, how would they be able to stop between rounds? (They couldn't.) How could hockey players, after having a bench-clearing brawl, possibly be able to shake hands afterwards, and leave it on the ice? (They couldn't.) But, because of outstanding control of their killer instinct, they can make a living from a natural reaction that would otherwise land them in prison.

Allowing your killer instinct to go unchecked will only hurt you. Those people who choose not to keep the killer instinct in check are those who fight more than they need to (they go looking for trouble). Those who pick on others for satisfaction, or those who go one step beyond and break the law, have allowed the killer instinct to devour them.

In class situations (sparring), the killer instinct should be exposed in short, controlled bursts. Once your attack has hit its mark, your opponent is dazed, you sense victory, you step in to finish the opponent, then step back and relax. You bring the killer instinct back inside and put it to rest until needed again.

In street situations, the killer instinct serves two purposes. It allows the fighter to finish his opponent to the point of unconsciousness (because on the street you can never be too careful), and it can be used to override fear.

Because the street is not a controlled situation, many times fear will seize the fighter. When dealing with fear one thing must be remembered: *fear has no power over the killer instinct*. Fear is a result of situation. The killer instinct is an inbred impulse to terminate whatever has caused it to be awakened. Once released, it will subdue any minor or major emotional irritation, even fear, if that emotion has proven to be uncontrollable.

Though it may sound as if the killer instinct is a dangerous thing, it is in fact an invaluable asset to any martial artist. It can push you to levels you never thought possible, and it can keep you safe when other areas of training may fail. For those in the martial arts realm who find themselves without the killer instinct, the only suggestion I can offer is that of emotional fortification, which, if trained properly, is the closest you will come to the killer instinct. But it may be close enough.

Training

Time. It comes, it goes. What we choose to do within these limits is totally up to us. Sleep in, party hard, ignore responsibility...whatever the choice, one thing is certain: it all comes out in the wash and nothing can run from the continuation of existence. The martial arts, though mystical and boundless, must also answer to the portals of time. Because of this, what you do with your "martial art" term is essential. Broken down to its basics, time is: moments spent training to the point of excellence.

The single most important element in your martial arts journey is training. It is this element that is most responsible for the expertise you will reach in your chosen style. Training will not only guide and influence your entire martial arts perspective, but will allow you to get an immediate grasp of how to interpret information.

Though it should be understood that training is a very personal thing, and not everyone will comprehend a chosen style as quickly as another, there are some aspects of this area that should be discussed.

Because the training realm can be as complicated or as simple as you make it, and because you have entered a new world (or are looking for a change in the shape of the present one), the guidelines for training may vary from person to person, but there is some common ground.

This chapter should not be looked upon as "The Commandments," but rather as a helpful outline for someone trying to organize a training routine or trying to revise their old system.

General Training

Training At Your School (Club, Dojo)

It should be understood immediately that the bulk, if not all of your technical knowledge, will be taught to you at your school. The martial arts club is the one area within which the rawness of your style will be exhibited. Training in a group situation calls for attention, seriousness, and respect for the instructor.

Because there are so many different personalities in a group and because not everyone will learn at the same speed or level, more things can distract an instructor or student.

You must remember that club time is for the study of pure technique. If you want to excel, then you must do nothing to interrupt the class. Most clubs will have a set of techniques or specific exercises that all practitioners do either to warm up or to prepare for the teaching of more advanced movements, but even during this interval all students should be readying their minds for the forthcoming techniques.

Though it is very refreshing for an instructor to see a friendship develop between his students, "schmoozing" should be done only before and after class.

Many times practitioners who find themselves "gifted" and ahead of the rest of the group will try to break away from the student core. This is unsatisfactory. Not wanting to train with the core group is insulting, not only to the other students who are involved, but to the instructor as well. When an individual breaks away, thoughts through the rest of the group will become individualistic: "If she can do that, then so will I." This type of thinking will destroy class concentration and students' readiness to listen to the instructor. Who wants to have respect for someone who allows a junior to ignore him—and once an instructor loses his students' respect, a club downfall is inevitable.

There is, however, a strength to group learning—the power of the catalyst. It is human nature to compete (healthy competition). This desire for competition can be used to the club's advantage as long as the instructor doesn't allow the catalyst to become disdainful.

The beauty of the human spirit is in pushing others to excel, and in the case of the martial arts training class, this could be a most beneficial tool. If each student pushes the others to surpass previous aptitude in the style, then the group (although composed of individuals) will become a well-oiled machine concerned with only one goal—perfect techniques. This will allow for a longer learning curve and will also energize the instructor and create a solid club alliance.

Because group training is the first type of discipline a new martial artist will encounter, it will also shape training habits in other fields (i.e., training with a partner or by yourself).

Whatever the outcome, training with a group will definitely cement in your mind the type or method of training you prefer, and that in itself will catapult you to the next level of fighting prowess.

Training with a Partner

Once you have become efficient in group situations, it is not surprising that the next step will be to pair off with only one partner. This is the transition from shadowboxing to actual physical contact, and it is often an eye-opening experience.

Frequently, a person who believes himself to be quite efficient at certain beginning techniques is paired off with a partner and finds that, when trying to execute techniques on a moving target, things do not go quite as he had imagined they would.

Finding out that a technique is not as easy as it appears to be while shadowboxing should show you that learning a style of martial art is a slow process that must be studied from all aspects.

Pairing off with another individual should be used for technique breakdown. Do not get into the habit of "pulling" your techniques, but rather use your partner to increase your awareness of both technique and your fighting zone.

The *fighting zone* is the area in which an individual feels most comfortable. This would include distancing, style of fighting, and even attitude. Studying with a partner increases the total awareness of this zone. To achieve the knowledge of the fighting zone, one must first develop and understand their *point of danger*—that area in which a fighter feels that physical retaliation is warranted. Each person in the world has his own idea of how much space is required for safety and comfort (personal space), and the only real way to fully comprehend this is by training with another person.

Unlike shadowboxing, a partner can push you past the average learning curve. Basically, your mind works more than usual to take in all the data and then store it in the appropriate files. When your mind becomes comfortable, or even content with an idea or feeling, it reduces drive for improvement. This can be seen in everything, including the martial arts. You join a club or dojo in hopes of becoming an outstanding fighter. You train day and night, hour upon hour, in the pursuit of perfection. However, many times something happens along the way: complacency— and soon to follow, loss of "hunger."

When an athlete loses "the hunger," he boards a downward spiral to nowhere. So many times a person who wishes to become a great fighter falls into this trap. He begins to see himself as fully evolved in the martial arts, and feels that he can learn no more.

This feeling of completion can be linked to many things, but the biggest of these are what are known as *plateaus*. A plateau can strike at any time, any level of training. It can be compared to a "writer's block" or a weight lifter's "max," and has claimed the training life of many a martial artist.

Plateaus are especially dangerous in the martial arts, not because of the stress they cause, but rather because of the illusion they create. Because the martial arts are so diverse, a plateau can be misinterpreted to mean incomplete styles or to mean an immediate need to combine disciplines. This can not only lead you astray, but take away your faith in a given style. Plateaus should not be looked upon as unfavorable but as an evolutionary step. A plateau means upgraded skill. You train in order to improve. However, your mind will need sufficient time to truly digest all of the lessons, so when your mind feels that the time has come to break down all the thoughts, it will magically lower the learning curve to make way for input breakdown. Once all previous lessons have been digested, the learning curve will be reinstated, and you will see improvement once again.

You cannot avoid a plateau, but you can partially control its length of time. As some martial artists will tell you, some plateaus can last for a year or more. This is hard on the student, as well as the teacher.

The most beneficial aspect of training with a partner, aside from technique understanding. is *plateau manipulation*. Training with a partner will increase the input breakdown of the brain. It will help explain things quickly and easily, and your mind will accept data more readily when it works in unison with instinct and feeling.

Once you sense the arrival of a plateau, you should immediately begin to work with a partner not only to decipher information, but also to interject a new environment for your mind to call upon for information breakdown.

Partner training increases sense of timing, distancing, and fear of an opposing force. It allows both you and your partner to get a feel as the defender and attacker. Because the two (defending and attacking) are so different, it is healthy training for you to have experience in both. The beauty of this type of training is the *reversal effect*. You may find that through being an attacker, certain revelations dealing with defending will occur. Because your mind is concentrated on attacking, your subconcious mind now begins to figure out strategies of the opponent. What is the opponent doing? Defending.

So, in a small sense, when you are in the attacking mode, another part of you will be in the defending mode in hopes of outsmarting your rival. The same is true when you take on the role of the defender. Although you are in a defensive role, your inner mind has started to think of attacking techniques to try to psychically intercept the attacker's motions.

Defender/attacker training with a partner will probably do more for your fighting character than any other single training tool. It must be understood, however, that this should not be defined as "sparring," but rather as a set of systematic attack and defense scenarios.

In partner training, active communication is very important. It is up to your partner to tell you your strong and weak points. Because of the importance of this, egos should be left at the door. You and your partner should strive only for improvement. If direct competition is your goal, then pick a partner against whom you have no competitive urges. This will be your best association.

Take notes about your partner's motions during both attack and defense. These notes are for your benefit as much as they are for him. Reveal what you saw and felt, hold nothing back. If you can articulate his strong points, then it proves your understanding of the style in question, as well as your proficiency in the techniques. If you can spot weak points, then it shows your ability to pick up on bad habits and increases your *aggressive timing*.

Partner training must be a two-way street. Be prepared to criticize and be criticized. Welcome suggestions from your partner. Ask how your power or your speed helps or hinders the technique. Are you telegraphing anything? Does your attack lack an element? Does your defense flow smoothly? Don't be afraid to ask questions. This will be the only time an attacking force will sit down and help you—the next time it could be for real. The major quality that separates a good fighter from a great one is knowledge of self, and the best way to learn about yourself is through the eyes, ears, and mind of another.

Training Alone

Another misunderstood training tool is time spent alone. Because the martial arts are so specific in both technique and culture, the lesson has not stopped when you go home, although technically it should have.

Physical conditioning

The biggest problem that young or new martial artists have is themselves. So many times a practitioner will learn a set of movements and then rush home to practice them. Though many would look upon this as great dedication (which is true), in reality, it is detrimental to the teaching process.

When a teacher gives a new movement to you to learn, it should be understood that it will take time for the technique to be fully accepted by your mind, and little subtleties must be checked and rechecked. Though this applies more to new students than to the more experienced, everyone will always be learning and therefore no one will never know it all.

When you go home and practice a new technique without the watchful eye of the instructor, the proper corrections cannot be made. Therefore mistakes and improper movement will not be corrected and bad habits will infect the technique. This results in the instructor having to work doubly hard to undo the now inbred mistakes that have occurred at home.

Once a mistake has become inbred, the instructor not only has to override the natural learning curve, but also has to deal with an element that wasn't there previously. It is because of this that training at home should be in a realm totally away from martial art technique and form.

Training alone should encompass something that does not involve procedure, but rather conditioning. Many times a practitioner will spend hours practicing a movement or sequence of movements, but the physical ability to perform these movements is lacking. Simply stated, the body is in no shape to execute what the mind is ordering.

Martial arts conditioning is a much-neglected aspect of training because too much time is spend on technique perfection. However, if a certain area of training were to be assigned specifically for conditioning, this problem could be solved.

Solo training should deal with conditioning of the martial artist. It does not rely on supervision or strive for technique perfection, and in reality does not have to be taught. Areas such as endurance, strength, and speed can be set aside for home training. This gives the club or dojo a special duty and the times away from the club a focus.

Running, weights, swimming, or any physical exercise, when done properly and on a regular basis, can only help a martial artist's ability. Aerobics, skipping, or even exercise videos can accelerate a martial artist to levels of "total performance."

When club time ends, then your technique practice should be over as well. But this in no way means that your training day has to end. For as much as the mind had to work in the learning of a martial art, the body must work twice that to allow the proper strength and flexibility needed to perform the techniques in question.

Mental conditioning

However, endurance training is not all one can do to better themselves in their chosen discipline. Another major component of the "total" martial artist is mental conditioning.

Mental conditioning can be explained as *the total readiness the mind exhibits when forced to execute a task that has become instinctual or subconcious.* When dealing with the martial arts, mental conditioning will allow the mind to react to a situation rather than having to "manually" think out a strategy.

When learning the martial arts, there are numerous exercises, techniques, and forms all created for the advancement of the style or art in general. Every style will have distinctions, but all will strive to teach fighting prowess and culture.

However, there is a huge difference between knowing hundreds of techniques and knowing when to execute those techniques, and the one thing that will narrow that margin is proper mental training.

Because mental training takes place inside your mind, it should be common sense that it should be done alone. Mental training will add that extra element that will push you to a new level of consciousness.

There are numerous ways to train the mind. However, because you would not want to readily initiate actual physical movement (so as not to create any bad habits that the instructor will later have to correct), *mind scenarios* or *mind sparring* may be practiced.

Mental sparring is relatively easy to initiate. All you need to do is sit in a comfortable position, and mentally set up an area, an atmosphere (dark, foggy, etc.), and attackers (three is a good starting point).

Once everything is set up, simply imagine the fight. Deal with the attackers in any way, shape, or form. One thing that you should notice: when a technique is performed in your mind, the stances, techniques, timing, and power usage are perfect. You must never imagine yourself as clumsy or unskilled.

What this training does is allow your mind to play with all the combative information that it has stored up since the beginning of training. Then, the imagination gives your mind a situation, and, almost like a computer, your mind has time to assess and distinguish which techniques are good for what.

Try the following assignment: for the next three days, 15 minutes a day, sit and imagine yourself in a fighting stance. Then imagine an individual standing in front of you, fists clenched. Now imagine this attacker lunging at you, and you slap away his hand and counter with a well-placed elbow to the side of the head. For the entire time, imagine this over and over and over again. Then, after the three days, grab a partner from your club. Ask them to attack you with one of three things; a kick, a grab, or a lunge. Though there are no guarantees, two out of your three defenses may more than likely be an elbow strike.

What your mind has done is pick out the best time for an

elbow attack based simply on visualization. Through this visualization, your mind has decided the proper stance, weight displacement, and power expenditure, and it is now easier for those decisions to be transferred to actual physical motion.

Another visualization technique is *tele-fighting*. What you can do is sit in front of the television and watch a boxing match, or kickboxing, or any activity that has a lot of physical movement.

You will then single out one participant and focus on his body movements. After a few minutes of studying, you should begin to call out the movements of the participant. Through a transitional period, you should eventually be able to call out the participant's movement before they are actually executed. This allows your mind to digest body movements and rhythm, so as to be able to foresee the most logical attacks or defenses of an opponent.

Mental conditioning is as important as any other phase of training to a martial artist. By preparing the mind, you can accelerate your learning process. Techniques will become more instinctual, and it allows for more advanced techniques to not only be easily understood but more readily injected into the subconcious mind for later use.

You should do your mental training in a nonclass environment, and you should be alone. Avoiding distractions will give you better concentration so as to allow your mind to fully study the body's conditioning, abilities, and of course readiness to execute techniques. In short, mental conditioning is the stage in which a fighter can build up the inside, the area that houses the most defects in the martial artist.

Training with Forms

Though many martial artists do learn the forms of their chosen style (set pattern of movements for both empty hand and weapons), most do not realize the incredible potential of those forms.

Though most practitioners feel that forms were created to pass on the look and feel of the style, you should remember that all the movements used to create these forms are fighting movements. The major rule to keep in mind when dealing with the forms is to know the purpose of each movement.

Each action in a form must have a purpose, and it is the responsibility of both the student and the instructor to understand the purpose of all. One must realize that when in actual combat, a practitioner WILL NOT FIGHT IN FORM. What this means is that although each movement in a form is for combat, the way they are strung together to create a form is not necessarily the way they will be executed when fighting.

Each movement of each form should be studied and understood. In this, an individual who has problems with the "controlled" elements in sparring can become as deadly a fighter, if not more so, than one who spars every day.

Forms give a fighter rhythm, style, and grace. They create a timing based on an individual's size, and shape, but the major attribute of forms training is an understanding of combative movements. Forms training, when broken down and studied, is the purest type of martial arts training because the movements have been passed down from generation to generation.

When dealing with weapons forms, the thought process should be no different. Like the hands, weapons are just extensions of the arms and legs, and training should be conducted as such. Just because you have a stick in your hands doesn't mean that you should abandon all training and instincts of hand techniques. Rather, the stick should now become a part of the body, flowing along with every other movement. It should not stop combat messages from the mind, but rather create and increase thoughts.

Once you grab a weapon, you should realize that there are now vast areas of distancing and rhythm that can be expressed. The beauty of training with weapons forms is that they don't take away or detract from the style in any way—they just add to it.

For example: A Tae Kwon Do stylist (who employs more kicking than hand techniques) should not abandon his kicking prowess just because he now has a staff or sword in hand. So many times, a person will ignore the whole foundation of his style just because an alien element is introduced. With regards to our example, once a staff is involved, the Tae Kwon Do stylist finds himself firmly planted on the ground, swinging the staff awkwardly, and probably feeling completely useless.

Why would practitioners ignore the positive aspects of themselves just to accommodate a piece of wood? The answer—they shouldn't. Because of the style's foundations, your mind and body know everything needed to perform perfect kicks: the staff should only assist in the eventual launching of those techniques. An off-balance thrust should become a catalyst to a deadly roundhouse or aerial kicking technique. Many may think that this would be impractical, but why would you give up 100 percent kicking prowess for 25 percent staff fighting prowess? By keeping to the instinctual kicking style, the two new techniques (kicking and staff fighting) will fuse to eventually create a new method of combat.

Granted that this will take many hours of training, but if you treated each discipline separately, it would take double the training hours. By sticking to the strength of the style studied, the total number of training hours will be far fewer and your confidence level will be greatly magnified.

You should realize that when dealing with a flowing activity such as the martial arts, you cannot put a specific mathematical label on it. However, training from your "style foundations" can speed the learning process and increase your prowess in a shorter length of time without sacrificing form or techniques.

Agents of the Martial Arts

The Punch

Probably the simplest, most effective weapon of the martial arts is the punch. It is simple in origin as well as in usage. It is because of this simplicity that it has the high effectiveness ratio that it does. Training your punch can be as personal as selecting the clothes you buy. The training should encompass speed, accuracy, and power. For speed training, you should try to punch at an object that has little or no resistance, such as a twig, a piece of paper, or curtains. When an object has no resistance, it lets your mind work on getting the punch there quickly without having to move the object. Accuracy training should be quite similar except that there should be numerous targets at different levels so as to challenge the eye/hand coordination circuitry. Power training is simple—use a heavy bag.

Because the punch is more readily called upon than any other martial arts technique, it should be versatile. Always know where it is going and always know the feeling of the power and speed equality that is necessary for a good punch. Keep an eye on extension, and always use flurries rather than single movements.

The Jab

When training the jab (in both boxing and other martial arts), speed is very important. Jabs are more of a set-up movement or a technique to keep opponents off balance so that they are unable to get going. A speedy jab can allow you not only to launch an attack, but, because of its speed, to recover quickly from a bad decision or even protect you when you are caught off guard. With regards to kung-fu, the jab has another purpose—it not only sets up other techniques, but it is more readily aimed at vital areas so as to cause damage and easy access for the next technique. Because of this, the fingers of the jab are outstretched and there is a lot of strength in the fingers. The fingers should have a slight bend in them to protect against injury and the thumb should be tucked to the side to avoid breakage.

For kung-fu jabs, an unusual but effective training method is to jab at a piece of light material (e.g., curtains, towels) and, without touching the material, make it move. When one is able to do this, it shows the true unison of speed and strength.

Blocking

Probably the mainstay of any style, whether it be kung-fu, karate, judo, or boxing, the block allows you time 1) to realize the distance from the opponent, 2) to get a good sense of the opponent's positioning, 3) to have time to execute a counter attack, and of course 4) to avoid injury.

Because many attacks require an intitiative by both combatants, it should not be surprising that the block will play a major role both defensively and offensively. Not only can the block begin initial movement in the launching of an attack or defense, but it can also set the rhythm and tone of the total encounter.

Blocks should not only be used to destroy an attack, but should carry with them a mind-set that will discourage the opponent. For instance, if an attacker throws what he feels is a confident and effective technique, but it is "seemingly" easily blocked, doubt may filter its way into the opponent's mind, and once doubt enters, the fighting spirit of the opponent begins to falter. Blocks should not only hurt the opponent physically, but mentally as well.

Confidence in blocking techniques will give you a depth of fighting that would otherwise be missed. That feeling of control while squaring off with another, whether they be friend or foe, can add to your total understanding of the martial arts. Blocking, like footwork, can give you a psychic link to all other styles because of the intricacies and simplicities, similarities and differences. Blocking makes a style whole, and serves as an effective tool for crossing over from one style to another. There are numerous ways to practice blocks, and each style will more than likely have their own. In this, each style keeps its practitioners unique, but also allows them to understand their techniques from both sides of the coin.

Grappling

One of the best tools for the understanding of weight displacement and opponent manipulation, grappling has found its way into many styles originally lacking in such close-quarters combat techniques. One of the main reasons for grappling is to increase the success potential when the combatants are too close for technical attacks or defenses.

Grappling, like blocking, will open you to new levels of thinking and understanding. The discipline of grappling is far more intricate than some arts simply because of the closeness of your enemy and, sometimes, the patience with which you need to achieve opponent domination.

Complete grappling styles such as judo and jiu jitsu strive for higher levels than most styles that just touch upon the realm, but this, of course, is due to the purity of the styles themselves.

For any martial artist, knowledge of his or her own body is essential for the total understanding of any fighting art. There is no law stating that just because a style may not incorporate grappling in its teachings, its students will never find themselves in a grappling situation.

Grappling should be described from simple wrist locks to the complex intricacies of jiu jitsu. Even in boxing, grappling has been utilized to allow a fighter to 1) save himself when fatigued, 2) stop the opponent's flurry of punches, and 3) give the boxer a chance to develop strategy. Grappling is probably one of the original styles of combat, and, although many would think that the larger of the combatants has the advantage, it all comes down to technique.

When a martial artist becomes knowledgeable about grappling, it immediately allows for different distancing methods. For example: a tae kwon do stylist will not feel so uncomfortable when fighting in a narrow hallway if he can fall back on some basic grappling skill. However, if this same fighter knew only the kicking techniques of the style, when forced to fight in the hallway situation, not only will he feel limited, but may even react to confrontation entirely out of fear.

This is not to say that a style of combat that has no grappling techniques is incomplete, but rather that its practitioners will have to travel outside the style to compensate for the absence. Grappling techniques should not be shunned or ignored, but eagerly researched for future use.

Kicking

Powerful, fast, and deadly, kicks are probably the most sought-after feature of the martial arts. The huge success of styles like tae kwon do, hap ki do, and, to an extent, even karate can be attributed to this appeal to young or beginning martial artists. One of the main reasons for this is probably the aerial kicks and the fast and powerful motions shown in the movies.

But kicks are as important as they are impressive. A kick can be simple—direct, swift, and powerful—or it can be intricate and still hold the same qualities of the simple kicks. Whether they are simple or intricate, kicks should be another added element for fighting rhythm, character, and timing.

If you do not possess proper timing, your kick will miss; without proper rhythm, your kick will be telegraphed; and without proper character, your kick will be sloppy and without form.

Like all of the agents of the martial arts, kicking is distinct within each style (omitting certain styles, such as western boxing, that have no kicking techniques).

Kicks can be used as set-up techniques, meaning that they can help maneuver the opponent into the desired position for a certain strike. They also can be used as *motion destroyers*, which basically means stopping an attacker's advance. Kicks could be *probing*—used as feints or feeling out an opponent's intended techniques.

When training kicks, you must have the purest understanding of both the kick and yourself. Everyone is different and you must know your range to successfully launch and connect with one of the kicking techniques. Because of leg length, sometimes you may find yourself having to add or subtract from a kick to achieve the effect. For instance, if you are about to throw a side kick, but realize that your opponent is too far from you, you may choose to add a little skip to compensate, or somehow move yourself closer to the target, so that the same technique can be thrown.

It is the above that makes kicking the best element for distancing training. A practitioner's range from an opponent has fooled many good martial artists and when their knowledge of distancing is not complete, their timing for technique as well as their range perception is hindered.

You should break your kicks down into certain groups. Again, please keep in mind that I have simplified the ranges as generally as I can, as I prefer not to dictate policy.

Breakdown

Short Range (e.g., shin-kick): body doesn't move, and kicking leg is barely extended.

Leg Range (e.g., side-kick): body doesn't move, and kicking leg is fully extended.

Long Range (e.g., flying side-kick): total body displacement and kicking leg is fully extended.

After you break down your range and begin to practice the three different lengths, (on a stationary object or with a partner) you will become very aware of both yourself and your target.

Once you become aware of distancing, your kicks not only become more efficient and effective, but all your other techniques will also benefit. The legs and knee should be like a probe, sending information to the mind so as to decide which technique to use based on a weakness your opponent has, or a habit he is falling into. You can register all of this once you know how to use your kicking techniques for more than just kicking.

Just remember that a kick should never travel alone or be expected to end the fight. Banking on one technique is dangerous, and some martial artists make the mistake of putting too much importance on one technique. Always string techniques together until your opponent is down and out. Remember, a kick is not just a technique, but also a gatherer of information, a relayer of false information, a strong image, or a helpless one. Whatever it is used for, be fully aware of its potential, and use it well.

Footwork

The way you travel from point A to point B can make or break a martial arts technique. Your mobility is probably the most important aspect of fighting. Because of this, footwork not only links you to your style, but can also aid in adapting to an opponent's style.

Of all the agents of the martial arts, footwork, although created from classical foundations, will be the most unique from fighter to fighter. Your stances and the way you manipulate yourself across space is as individual as your personality. One of the main reasons for this could very well be comfort. Because a martial artist wants to feel comfortable or in control when executing a technique, footwork is of the utmost importance.

Proper footwork and stances allow for explosion, speed, power, and, of course, accuracy. Without proper or developed footwork, you will never be able to fully understand or experience a pure technique. Your footwork should be as distinctive as your taste in clothes and food. Proper footwork is developed by feel.

When you want to experiment to find out what stances work best for you, you have to go through an elimination process. This process will encompass classical stances, weight displacement of legs, body angle, coiled or relaxed muscles, and hand placement—including southpaw or orthodox preferences.

Being in a stance is one thing, but getting there is usually the initial problem for a fighter. What you should do is practice getting into your stance from a walking motion. Walking is the most natural thing in the world, so all techniques or stances that will flow naturally should be easily executed from the walk. Once you find a stance with a certain degree of comfort, then the process should begin.

Dropping into a stance should be instantaneous. It should require no effort and the stance should not be too extended or contracted. That means the stance, for the sake of mobility, should be that middle ground between wide and erect stances. In the proper stance, a fighter should not feel aggressive or defensive but, rather, prepared. There should be no strain on any muscle, and the body should be as relaxed as possible.

Once you have chosen a stance, it is up to you to look for weaknesses and strengths within it. You can use a mirror to view leg position, center of gravity, and hand placement for attack or defense. You can also use a partner to scrutinize, make suggestions, or try out techniques.

The best way to gauge a good stance is speed. If you can explode out of a technique, or if your technique "flies" from the stance, chances are that the stance is complete. Mobility is another method of testing. When you feel able to move easily in any direction with both speed and balance, you probably have developed a good stance.

Although hand positioning may vary for different techniques, there should be a grey area where all techniques and stances fall into play. In this, a perfect stance and proper footwork will lead you to upgraded techniques, higher success ratio during attack, and increased space manipulation when being attacked.

Sparring

Sparring is the test between two independent minds, two independent skills. In almost every style you will find some form of exercise that is known as sparring. Two or more fighters pitting themselves against each other for the pure goal of improving fighting prowess.

As in everything else, sparring exercises should be molded to the wants of the practitioner. It is true that sparring is useful for the tournament scene—reflex training, discovery of subconcious technique, and the reading of body language. But sparring should not be the major training tool for an event that will encompass full-power, and uncontrolled situations, with the possibility of injury. In short, sparring may help in the area of controlled fighting, but if you want to better yourself for street survival, sparring is *NOT* the way to go.

Sparring should be used for testing speed, to see how fast you can get a technique off. It should help the martial artist realize rhythm and timing, but for actual combat (for which most styles seem to use it), sparring in my opinion, is unacceptable.

Sparring should be the forerunner of shadowboxing (when the fighter stands alone and uses full technique and power to destroy enemies that he has created in his mind). Sparring is fine for the first introduction to mobile targets (i.e., another living being and not a heavy bag), but it should not end there. When training with a partner, sparring should be controlled so as to benefit both parties. Sparring can help you learn which techniques are natural and help you notice habits that can give away a technique.

However, once you decide to prepare yourself for street combat, or once you've had your first combat in the street, sparring exercises should be discarded and you should then switch to the shadowboxing discipline.

Because sparring is controlled and performed with someone with whom the fighter is acquainted, certain fundamentals of real combat are lost. Sparring doesn't allow for fierceness, the execution of hurting techniques, or the evolution of the style. Mistakes in sparring may lead to a bruise or two…but mistakes in actual combat can lead to much more. (See Chapter 8, "Competition," for a more detailed analysis of this subject.)

For individuals only interested in the tournament circuit, sparring is probably one of the best training tools. Basically, tournament fighting is sparring. For a martial artist training for this area, always try to spar with someone obviously more skilled, but, more importantly, faster.

If you wish to better yourself in the sparring realm, you must spar out of your league. Sparring with an individual of equal or lesser skill will not be as productive.

As with all facets of the martial arts, sparring has its place. However, it should be up to both the teacher and student to realize that sparring is not law. What happens between two individuals in a school or dojo when sparring, in reality will have no bearing on actual combat. Work reflexes, play with techniques, learn speed and movement: these are the lessons of sparring. But for real combat, a fighter must step into himself and use everything learned and not hold back. He must try to manipulate emotions, know all techniques (their uses and functions), have perfect control of his body with both balance and rhythm. Sparring is only the first step to the conquering of an individual, not the final one.

Summary

Although all training exercises, whether it be with a group, alone, or with a partner, have characteristics of the style that has been chosen, and even though there will always be that search for individuality, always keep the honor of the style. While traveling through the training realm, look to the classical portion of your style to aid in the personalization. Do not abandon the teachings, for successful training is directly linked to the trust, honor, and the respect that you have for your martial art.

Competition

Many things about human nature make us very easy to predict. Anger, sadness, and other such emotions can usually be manipulated in one way or another. The mass media has this manipulation technique down to an art form. For example, if they wanted you to give money to save the grey wolf, you would see wolf puppies learning from their mother, playing, and exploring their world in a comedic or cute way. They might even show you some men killing puppies in order to further your sorrow. However, if the media wished for you to ignore the grey wolf plight, you would see packs of bloodthirsty wolves devouring an innocent creature (usually a fluffy and cuddly animal, like a rabbit); you would see how the wolves kill farmers' livestock and force farms to close down—well, I think you get the point.

When you learn something of a physical nature (though it can also come to those outside the physical realm), there is a driven force that propels us to want to test ourselves against others—it is in our nature to compete.

Competition comes in many forms, from good-hearted sporting games to savage world wars. The drive to be the best has always been there. In the martial arts, competition has probably ascended to the highest levels ever reached in modern times. Boxing, judo, and tae kwon do have found themselves listed among those revered physical contests in the Olympic Games, that have become the embodiment of pure competition. It is the martial arts pursuit of perfection that has brought about its incredible level of competition, and the level will continue to rise, as does the skill level of the arts themselves.

The hours of training put in by an individual in any given discipline usually leads to the one area that gives immediate gratification—the tournament scene.

No matter what the style, most branches of the martial arts hold events that will allow individuals to test their skill against those of another. The tournament scene should not be confused with the testing of realistic fighting prowess—they are for display and testing of skills learned over the years.

The beauty of tournaments is the allowance of pure technique of a given art to be shown. Whether it be in hand forms, weapon forms, or sparring, tournament events allow one to see why the fighting styles are called arts.

When preparing for a competition, you must look closely at the format of both presentation and judgment. These are the two areas that can make you win or lose a competition.

Always keep in mind that a tournament is your chance to represent both your school and your style of martial art. It should be in this thought that you find your desire and your drive to do your best.

With regards to the three areas of competition, one must prepare for each in a slightly different way.

Hand Forms

The hand forms (shadowboxing) are sets of movements put together that allow a practitioner to become comfortable with a number of techniques at one time. The individual movements are linked together to create an almost rhythmic motion of combat, with the only difference being the lack of opponents.

Because hand forms are displayed personally, all the attention is on the practitioner. This is probably the main reason for the need for power and focus in a set. A form without power or focus makes the performer look confused and insecure.

The main thing to remember in form presentation is the beginning and end. These are the two elements that the judges are sure to remember.

When you approach the judges, walk with a purpose, holding your head up high and proud. Do not confuse this with arrogance. A proud martial artist will get respect from the judges, and that will be evident in the final mark.

Your beginning presentation must capture the judges' immediate attention. You have to keep them watching you at all times, you must convince them (nonverbally) that if they continue to watch you, they are going to see the greatest form ever. They should be concerned about missing even the simplest salute, because if you can get the judges to believe this, your form will already look better.

Obviously, the actual contents of the form (the initial moves) do hold merit. They must be executed with power and conviction, without pause or confusion. They should be crisp with structure and fluidity. One way to train is to visualize the form in your mind.

The beauty of mind training is the form in which you see yourself. As discussed in Chapter 7, when you imagine yourself executing a martial arts technique, the form is perfect. Also, in mental imagery you will continue to inject the movements into your subconscious, so that actual thinking of the movement is not needed. You know a form is in you if you can think of other things while performing it.

If, for some bizarre reason, you find that you have made a mistake in your form, DON'T STOP! Remember, the men and women judging you are more than likely from different schools; they don't know the moves, or what order they are in, so, unless you make obvious facial gestures or stop in the middle of a form, no one but yourself will realize that a mistake has been made. Continue as if nothing has happened and you may not be docked points.

A final suggestion regarding the core movements of the form concerns the facial expression. Your face will say a lot about you. With regards to performing a set, one should look mean—snarl! Many times the judges will look to your facial expressions to see how comfortable you are with a set. If you look like you're thinking about the movements, they may dock you.

You may think that a mean facial image falls under the judgment of focus. It does not. Focus is the actual completion of a movement; sharp, powerful, good entry into the move, and good transition into the next. Snarling and looking fierce (maybe even growling or making noise), will magnify your focus, but it gives the judges an image of mind and body unity—something that calls for good marks.

The ending of a form is an area in which most tournaments are won or lost. So many times a practitioner will be so "gassed" up for the performance, that by the end they are so tired that they can't finish the set or the final moves look sloppy.

Remember, your last moves, as well as your salute and exit from the competition area, are the judges' last impression of you. To ensure their good marks along with their respect, finish strong. This can be accomplished with a final burst of strength, extra strong stances, and a powerful vocalization on the final move. Also, when you salute, hold it a little longer than usual. What this does is force the judges to give you a mental mark immediately, while your impression is positive. Then remember to walk off the competition area with strength and pride and keep eye contact with the judges until the last possible moment.

Weapons Forms

Once the precision of hand combat has been attained, it is time to test one's coordination with the addition of a new element—a weapon.

The beauty of a weapon form is to see the unity between the practitioner and the weapon itself. There is nothing more stimulating to the eye than a person taking a foreign object and turning it into an extension of the body.

When competing, as in hand forms, the competitor must enter and finish strong. However, one difference between the weapon and hand form competitions is the content, meaning that a weapon form competition may be won by an impressive movement within the set, something that will stand out, something the judges will remember. Because of this added element, a lot of weapon competitors try to cash in on that one fanciful movement in hopes of swaying the judges.

Whether or not that is the determinant in winning competitions, what you should train for is perfection. Don't rely on one segment in a form to win—use it all. Concentrate, fully understanding your weapon, fully understanding each movement, and use the weapon as if it were an appendage.

As in hand form competitions, complete all movements, look fierce, and be sure to leave a lasting impression.

One trick in getting a weapon to become second nature is to play with it—not in form or tactic—just play around with the weight, the size. Make up moves, get to know the "spirit." Until you do this, your attempts to master its movements will be incomplete.

Comfort or awkwardness with a weapon can be seen immediately, not only by the judges, but the spectators and, more importantly, the other schools. Remember the pride for your school, make your instructor proud—that will be the biggest trophy of all.

Sparring

In dealing with preparation of tournament sparring techniques, you must first realize that both the nerve of the participant as well as his emotional stability are not as consequential as some may think.

When dealing with competition, the above-mentioned should not be a major factor for two reasons. First, it is a test of skill: if a person loses, it should indicate that the opponent's skill was, at that moment, superior. Second, sparring in a tournament is a controlled situation. As opposed to the street, the tournament scene is a relatively safe environment in which to practice and display martial arts abilities. You should realize this, and take full advantage.

Basically, fighters should have two frames of mind: *Realistic*, the true presence of danger and need to preserve their life; and *Abstract*, the realization that the events occurring are fabricated to help a practitioner advance their martial art skills. In the tournament circuit, sparring definitely falls into the second category. Granted, you are putting your skills up against another individual, and granted that an opponent's strike may cause pain (perhaps even a minor injury), but it is a controlled situation—there really is no danger.

In tournaments, you should realize that if you get knocked down or get in some sort of combative trouble, there will be a third party (referee or judge) to step in and halt any and all actions.

The most common mistake plaguing fighters today is their failure to separate sparring from actual combat. When preparing for combat in a controlled situation, the frame of mind of a fighter should be different than that of street combat. Because of the distinct difference between the two, there are numerous skilled street fighters that, if they entered a tournament, wouldn't make it past the first round. On the other side of the coin, the same can be said of tournament fighters. It would be possible to see the most skilled tournament champion defeated in a street fight by a mediocre street fighter—frame of mind!

Sparring should be looked upon as a type of experiment. Think of it, a controlled situation with no life-threatening danger—a perfect time to play around with technique. Tournament sparring allows form. This is not to say that the sparring in tournaments must have fixed positions and stances, but, because both

90

fighting parties are there for skill investigation, the chances for traditional technique will be greater.

Literally, tournament sparring is more like a game of tag. Always remember that speed beats power in sparring competitions. So when preparing for a tournament, make your moves simple but fast. Work on reaction time, move in and out quickly, while at the same time striking—always train for the event. Sparring requires quickness, so quickness training should be tops on the list. And, because intricate techniques take too long, SIMPLE IS BEST.

Bag work, shadowboxing, and sparring with a partner are all acceptable for tournament preparation. But to truly be successful, you must go one step beyond the physical and tap into the one resource that has infinite vitality—the mind.

Train to take advantage of the rules, attack without hesitation. Most participants seem to be leery when confronted in a tournament, but, in reality, what is there to be lost? The match, but that is all. This should be a strength. There is no danger to you, so attack with confidence. Keep good concentration and form—there are no worries about outside forces (e.g., hidden weapons, surprise attackers), and because of this, your mind can be clear and set on the individual standing across from you.

The only training you must do for tournament fighting is to allow your mind to open up all avenues and have confidence. Once you can train your mind to understand the lack of danger in a tournament situation, the magic of reflex, instinct, and drive to win will override everything else. This is the mark of a true champion.

Tradition

Tradition, usually embodied as a long-established custom or practice that has the effect of an unwritten law, or any of the usages of a school of art or literature handed down through the years, may be the only saving grace for the "old style" martial arts.

A decision to study a martial art will not only involve a willingness to undergo physical domination, but cultural submersion as well. To truly be one with your style, you as the practitioner must become familiar with the area or culture from which it came. Most martial art traditions stem from the country of their origin, and even if you are not of that country, the "old way" should be observed.

You are not actually surrendering to the culture, but instead assuming some of its values in an effort to dissect your style. Anyone who has studied Chinese kung-fu will tell you that, until you do a *Lion Dance*, the true appreciation of the intricate footwork will be lost. The power of the lion comes from its movement. The power of kung-fu combat comes from its motion, its quick mobility and from its footwork.

Stepping outside the fighting ideals and learning your style's culture will open your mind to an extra facet of inward thinking. Why are we awed by a certain martial art? Because it seems magical. This magical respect leads us to want to study it. Then, when we learn that a punch is just a punch, we have even more respect for a chosen style because of the beauty it displays in execution of such a simple technique. So too, for cultural and traditional beliefs. At first they seem weird and excessive, but when you take the time to study their personal meanings and symbols, you are thrown into a world as impressive as the martial arts themselves.

Identity can be expressed by many things. But one of the most influential of these is, of course, tradition. This can range from ways of dressing or speaking, to even dancing. Whatever the tradition, one thing is certain—it has been preserved to further the heritage in question. Giving a sense of pride allows a heritage to instill in its members the desire to stay pure, not wanting to modernize just to match the ever-changing society of which it is a part. This allows for ancient ideals to survive undisturbed and allows future generations the chance to experience the beauty of an age-old culture.

When talking of martial arts, one must realize that the subject in question spans numerous cultures. There is kung-fu (Chinese), karate (Japanese), tae kwon do (Korean), savate (French), arnis (Filipino), capoeira (Brazilian)—the list goes on and on.

With culture comes tradition, and with tradition comes pride. As a practitioner of an art, one must realize that there will be some sort of unwritten do's and don'ts. This is not to say that the culture is trying to change you in any way, but rather it is asking you to understand and respect the ideals and principles of its ways.

Martial art clubs, more than any other, will be strict about their traditions, because it is these traditions that make the club and style complete. What would happen if a karate student decided not to bow to his school's seniority, or a kung-fu school ignored the lion dance? The answer—loss of identity for both the culture and the school.

One word that could define the essence of martial art tradition is RESPECT. This encompasses all things. Is it not just the respect for the teacher, sifu, or sensei, but also respect for the school name, insignia, style, and so on. This need for respect is found in all cultures of the martial arts world, and it is the foundation of club and style success.

Martial arts tradition stems from history, and although society continues to change, the one aspect from the old world ingrained in these ancient arts is the esteem held for *experience, age,* and *knowledge*. Because the respect for these three things stands at the pinnacle of martial prowess, it is not surprising that the cultures have given their own interpretation to the mystical term.

The regimentation of the Japanese arts is their source of honor. The worst thing you can do in a Japanese school is be disrespectful to your peers because, as in all martial arts schools, you are not only representing yourself but also your teacher and your style. If you are disrespectful, all eyes fall upon those who "created" you, and as a result they may not be looked upon favorably.

Understand that when you are in public wearing a shirt from your club or some article that displays your club's emblem, everything that you do reflects upon the club. If you're drunk and disorderly, those around you will get a bad impression of your club. If you are arrogant and bullying, the same. Just because you are outside your "training walls" doesn't mean that you are no longer responsible for the club's image.

At the beginning of this chapter, we discussed culture. Going from one culture to another can cause trouble for the practitioner. Most times this is because of lack of understanding.

When studying an art, always be watchful. If there is something that you don't understand, ask. Most teachers will be more than happy to share their cultural diversities; it's part of being a teacher. Ask about the lion dances, the incense burning, the bowing to idols—find out why you are doing it and what it represents. In this you will not only further your acceptance in your style and club, but solidify your martial arts presence within the school's pecking order.

Never go against the grain. If new students are made to sweep the floor before class, this is what should be done. The exercise is not to humiliate, but rather to carry on a tradition that probably originated with the style's creator.

Traditions will give more of a sense of identity than any other facet of the martial arts. They are your time tunnel back to the very beginnings of your style. We should all be grateful for knowing a style's history and the proper acts of respect that have come from a different origin in both time and place. All these things should and will propel you forward, and allow for injection of your personality and present-day ideas. Basically, the thought behind tradition was for preservation; in reality, it just may be the key to the continued evolution of the fighting arts as a whole.

Learning tradition will also affect the most important of all areas of the martial arts, the instruction. Becoming an instructor not only gives you the responsibility for passing on techniques and personas, but also adds the chore of maintaining the incorporation of regimentation of a thousand years ago into present-day society. It is your duty to understand your style's traditions for no other reason than that of "passing on the flame." Young minds need guidance and old minds need understanding. To complete both these tasks (usually at the same time, and in the same class), the intricate knowledge of folklore, myth, history, heroes, villains, martyrs, and the successes and failures of your chosen style will allow you, as the "all knowing" sifu (or sensei, etc.), to keep that image. Keep the wide-eyed student wide-eyed and constantly hungry for knowledge.

Finally, there is another aspect of the martial arts that is sometimes overlooked, or even shunned, because of the uncertainty of the answer—the rules regarding when to fight. Though you may frown, this subject does fall under the "tradition" aspect of a martial art. Because many traditions extend from beliefs, in a martial arts club the "when to fight rules" are clearly outlined. These beliefs are learned through experience, and not through word of mouth. Though some schools may vary slightly, there are basically five reasons for combat (though your order of importance may vary, the following is my breakdown):

1. To protect yourself
2. To protect family
3. To protect those who cannot protect themselves
4. To protect your teacher
5. To protect the honor of your school and style

Traditions are upheld for distinct reasons. For some clubs it is their link to the old country, whereas for others it is the way it has always been done and it maintains purity of the style. For some it is a way to show would-be students the authenticity of the club.

Whatever the reason may be, traditions are as much a part of the martial arts as a punch or kick. Look upon them with intrigue and follow them down to the fine lines of respect. For only in doing so can you ever hope to achieve true mastery of your style and your new-found life.

Cross-Training

No matter what is to be said about any activity in our lives, movement is movement and motion is motion. It's generally thought that our bodies achieve a certain frame of movement at a very young age. This individualistic style of motion allows certain individuals to excel at certain challenges that others may deem as out of their realm of talent.

Though there could be some thread of truth to that notion, natural movement can to some extent mold itself into another form or shape. This is to say that, if someone is a very poor hockey player, for example, he should look to his natural movement and then approach his sport from the strength of individual motion. In that way, the chances of increasing his skill is much more likely.

If broken down to the simplest forms, there is no difference between a hockey player, football player, baseball player, dancer, or marathon runner. Of course the actual movement and motion used by each in their respective sports will differ, but the precision with which they must train their bodies to work in that needed manner will be the same.

A hockey player practices and studies his stroking motions on the ice. The football player concentrates on natural explosion of the muscles, lateral movements, and body deception and trickery. The baseball player focuses on hand and eye coordination to get the perfect swing at the ball, the perfect pitch, and the fiery throw to the plate. The dancer practices circular motions and controlled extensions of the arms and legs. The marathon runner uses maximum form to achieve the endurance and focus needed to travel such long distances.

Looking at each sport in this manner, though the style of training as well as intensity may vary from sport to sport, one detects a common thread in the maximum efficiency of the needed movement to perform the task at hand.

If all the attributes from these sports are collected, we would find power, balance, muscle explosion, lateral movement, body deception, hand-to-eye coordination, circular motions, appendage extensions, endurance, and focus. Each of these given attributes can be found within the foundations and styles of the martial arts.

Though many people might stamp and kick their heels at my analogy, I look upon any and all sports as *chewing a stick of gum*. My reasoning for this is simple. When the body and mind becomes comfortable with an idea or movement, it becomes content. Content to me means complacency, and complacency means stagnation. Though many people will not want to hear this, we as human beings are naturally lazy. This means that our minds and bodies, when familiar with a task or idea, will find the easiest way to perform or translate this chore. The mind and body will find every way possible to "cheat" the task so as to save energy, use less concentration, and find a way to relax.

Basically, what has happened is that the mind has successfully stored all the training information of a given sport in the proper areas of the brain and, with the body in correct shape to perform this information, the brain has all this leisure time.

Sports is like chewing a stick of gum; over a period of time, the flavor fades. The chewing of the gum becomes repetitive more than anything else, and sooner or later you toss the gum out. In the sporting world, the same thing has been seen countless times; an athlete trains, and trains, and trains, then one day—bang! He loses interest in the sport, his training habits dwindle, and eventually the athlete quits. The stick of gum has become so flavorless that he couldn't chew it any longer.

What he should have done, or might want to do, is rather than throw out that stick of gum, insert a fresh piece into the already flavorless one. The result is the fresh stick of gum reflavors the entire bulk. This reinstates a "tasty" rebirth for the athlete.

Any sports-minded person thinking of changing or reshuffling his sports training procedure may want to look to the martial arts for some sort of physical and mental "freshness." The bonus of the fighting arts is their capability to adhere to, or accomodate any and all forms of movement.

If you are an athlete, when you begin to feel stagnant in your sport, jumping into the martial arts would be the best "stick of gum" you could ever find. Not only would you be learning new ways to move or achieve the same goal as your sport might have, but you will have wakened the mind to new information that must be stored. This new duty for the brain will cause it to shift out of its "natural" lazy or cheating mode, and begin to call upon any and all resources to complete the new tasks that it has now been asked to do.

The beauty of a "direct injection" of the martial arts into your given sport is that the mind does all the work but the body benefits, as does the skill level of the sport in question.

The martial art injection will cause the brain to recall all the sporting information learned since the first time you picked up a hockey stick, baseball, or whatever. Why does it do this? Because the mind likes to learn from comfort and familiarity. And, because many of the motions and movements in the martial arts will have similarities to your already mastered sport, the mind falls back on what it knows, then adapts and improvises to meet the needs of the new physical performances.

This could be called a type of recircuiting, but I prefer to call it the *awakening of the giant*. I use this term because in my experience with athletes and their discovery of the martial arts as their cross-training tool, they explode into their given sport feeling ten feet tall and bulletproof.

A great example of this is my experience training three time World Figure Skating Champion Elvis Stojko. Many times throughout the training schedule I would travel up to Elvis' rink in Barrie, Ontario, to instruct him after his final skate in the afternoon. Though he would sometimes be fatigued from all his skating that day (sometimes between three to four hours), Elvis looked forward to the "freshness" of the martial arts and immediately would begin practicing the cross-training movements I devised. Because of his positive attitude toward cross-training, Elvis kept the intensity that he had on the ice and brought it with him to the training room. The result, as the workout moved on, he would get more and more energy and would crave more and more knowledge. By the end of the second hour, he was totally invigorated and ready for more. Now even though the lesson had ended, Elvis would mentally go over the exercises at home and figure out where they would fit into his training routine for the next few weeks. It was not surprising at all to get a call from Elvis the next day, telling me how well the cross-training exercises worked on the ice, and how he had come up with some new ideas of his own.

For over seven years now, I've made sure to give Elvis a fresh approach to his cross-training principles, mixing them with the raw energy of the martial arts. In doing this, it's very pleasurable to watch an already superb, high-caliber athlete continue to grow so much, both technically and spiritually, reaching that all important "next level." This is without a doubt cross-training in its purest form.

Although the bulk of this chapter has been dedicated to how the martial arts can help your performance in other sports, this in no way means that the martial arts themselves haven't benefited from the alliance. The injection of sporting information into a given martial art expands the martial art by giving it the opportunity to incorporate new ways to move and dominate an opponent. Because martial arts is an ever-forward mental state, the injection of sports situations allows the practitioner to call upon knowledge and instinct and mix it with improvisation.

A good example of this would be my first experience working with a professional roller hockey team. The exercises and martial arts drills were fine when we were all in track pants and running shoes, but when I switched to roller blades and hockey equipment my motion and movement were tested.

I have always believed that "if you can't do it—you shouldn't teach it." Because of this belief I designed a lot of my drills with the skates and equipment in mind. This accomplished two things: 1) I didn't insult the hockey team by teaching all off-ice drills with no consideration for their sport or the practical use within a real game, and 2) I gained their respect because I approached them as knowledgeable athletes who knew their sport much better than I did. I went to them with the intention of teaching, but also to learn.

As I discussed in earlier chapters, when incorporating something new into your mind you must learn from strength. Cross-
training is no different. While working with the hockey team I not
only stayed true to their sport, but when I encountered any diffi-
culty in passing along a technique or drill, I fell back to their
strength and the power of their familiarity. No matter what the
drill was, the goal was to put the puck into the net. As soon as I
incorporated that little detail into the exercises, the players picked
it up in minutes. The reason for this? They were moving on instinct
with one thing in mind—scoring. I taught from their strength.

In my teachings, I have noticed the excitement and intrigue
an athlete feels when he cross-trains with the martial arts for the
first time. But, so many times when I work with an accomplished
athlete, he feels that he must complete the "mental motions" of
the new drills within the time period that I'm there. For some reason (my guess is because he sees himself as the top level of sporting prowess) he feels that the cross-training principles and result
should come almost instantaneously. Well, it doesn't. When the
athlete becomes distressed by what he feels is a slow learning
rate, I describe the "cross-training/good meal" analogy.

When you eat a good meal, it tastes great. The main reason
you are enjoying this meal is simply because of the taste. But the
nutrients in the meal—the vitamins, minerals, proteins—take
time to work themselves through the body, and then, of course,
go where they are needed. Cross-training is no different. The initial days that the althete is taught is the eating of the meal. Then
he has to go home, relax, think about what he did, and review.

This is the digestion process, which requires time. Then the athlete will return to his main sport, and play and/or train to the best of his ability. Within this time, the cross-training drills will slowly involve themselves in the actual motion or movement of the sport—the nutrients are now being placed where they're needed.

Cross-training within the martial arts themselves should really follow the same guidelines as with sports. Be sure to use it to energize training in your chosen art, but also be sure to train from strength. Don't abandon your core style to learn another.

Cross-training your style with another has other obvious uses. Firstly, you can overcome any inconsistencies or weaknesses in your style by using the strong points of the chosen cross-training style. The example given earlier suggested the benefit of learning a grappling art for those who study a kicking style, and so on. Secondly, should you ever come in contact with a member of the style with which you have chosen to cross-train and it is a combative situation, you already have the upper hand. Chances are that they don't know your style, but you know theirs.

Another benefit to the cross-training of two fighting styles has nothing to do with combat at all, but rather image and judgment. When you go to another club or style, you are almost like an ambassador for your core fighting art. You are representing your school and instructor, and those you are visiting may very well use you as the guideline to their opinions of that style.

Though people hate to admit it, ego and arrogance have tainted much of the martial art world and perhaps even the sporting world in general. Everyone likes to think that their style of martial art, or their sport for that matter is the ultimate and none is better.

Karate looks down on kung-fu, kung-fu shuns wu shu, kicking styles scoff at grappling styles, and boxers look down on all that isn't boxing. This is all poisonous to the evolution of the arts. Sports have similar downfalls. Hockey players scoff at figure skaters, and figure skaters don't consider hockey skating proficient. Though the skating styles do differ in various ways, the performance of each separate sport's duties warrants the type of skating used by each. Though in any and all sports there is always room for improvement, we should perhaps give each other the benefit of the doubt.

Cross-training with the martial arts should be like a buffet of theories, drills, exercises, and routines. Take what is useful and leave the rest behind. There is no law that states that every aspect of the fighting arts can be adapted to a given sport or task, so don't force it. Your body knows what it needs, so listen to it. Never abandon the knowledge of your chosen sport—this is your translator for any and all physical motion you have yet to discover.

Breathing

There is one aspect of all motion and movement that stands universally: breathing. Without breath, there is no movement.

Proper breathing is probably one of the most ignored aspects of any and all exercise or sport. If used properly, breathing can push an athlete or practitioner to new levels of both endurance and performance. When handled poorly, breathing can make an athlete feel fatigued, confused, and totally separated from the body.

Many martial art schools have designated exercises to encompass the internal aspect of the training realm. When concentrating on the simple exchange of oxygen, breathing in through the nose and out through the mouth at a controlled rate is very common in the fighting arts.

Dynamic Tension is a set of exercises in which the practitioner uses muscle against muscle in an attempt to create an isometric environment. Within the tension of the exercise, the breathing principles are very simple. Breathe in on the relaxed preparatory movements, and exhale slowly with the tensed motions.

Dynamic tension can be used for more than just isometrics. The control and focus that it creates within the mind can be called upon at any time it is necessary. For example a hockey player can modify the breathing exercises to do some quick run-throughs while he is between shifts. A figure skater can use the exercises to collect all his energies right before he steps onto the ice to perform his program.

Martial artists will sometimes have a set somewhere within a form to give an added element of intricacy, as well as a point to re-energize, to finish the form in question. With something as natural to exercise as breathing, it can be accomodated almost anywhere.

Because kung-fu is my base style, the most basic form of dynamic tension is the *Eight Bridges*. Basically, the practitioner stands in a neutral "horse" stance and, with the dynamic strength in the arms ("dynamic" is defined as the controlled explosion of the muscles), moves them outward while exhaling. The arms move in eight different ways, hence the term.

When done properly and with the right focus, dynamic tension is a great workout. Not only can it serve to enhance your sport or martial art ability, it has been known to be a great cure for insomnia (practice a few sets just before you go to bed). Or as a stimulant (performing a few sets first thing in the morning, to get the blood moving).

Dynamic tension and focused breathing allows you to teach your mind and body to keep control even during stressful situations. Your usage of the air you breathe becomes more efficient and allows you to enhance performance of a given task with energy and vigor.

Chi kung is another form of breathing exercise that, like dynamic tension, concentrates on the usage of the oxygen in the body. However, chi kung goes a number of steps further in its usage, and has many more applications outside the realm of just breathing.

In the martial arts, it is believed that every person has an inner strength, a life force known in Chinese styles as *Chi*. This chi governs many things in both our body and our mind. Because of this importance, it should not be surprising that there would be some sort of exercises targeting that specific entity.

Chi kung exercises can range from the simple *Packing* (filling the lungs to full capacity, crunching the abdominal muscle for a number of seconds, then slowly and under control, exhaling) to the *Healing Sounds* (sets of breathing and packing exercises to regulate the body's internal workings, each having distinct characteristics in the exhaling area).

Visualization is another very powerful aspect of the chi kung family. In the martial arts for instance, a practitioner could stand in a shallow stance and go through his packing exercises, but added in are some basic visualization techniques to address a specific problem area. For example, a practitioner wants to work on his courage during stressful times or situations. Now, though the packing exercises will work on this automatically, with the added feature of actual visualization, the benefits can be more than doubled. All the practitioner need do is visualize on the inhale the breathing-in of clean breaths (courage), and on the exhale visualize dirty breaths (fear). This exercise should be performed over and over again until the alotted number of sets has been accomplished.

This is a form of recircuiting, because with the exercise at hand, when the practitioner comes into a stressful situation, one deep breath may be all it takes to remedy the fear or anxiety racing through his mind.

The most important thing to remember when practicing any breathing exercise is to be sure you have learned the technique properly, and be sure to NEVER OVERDO IT.

There is also a very important rule when dealing with breathing practice. When training, this is the time to think about what you're doing and break down the breathing techniques. But when performing your actual activity or playing your actual sport, the golden rule is BREATHE NATURALLY. Your body will know when to breathe and when to redirect. Don't think about it, just perform naturally. Just because you've practiced the dynamic tension or chi kung over and over in your workouts, when you're skating down the ice with the puck, or breaking through the bodies to catch that ball, let the body work naturally. The exercises will work as long as you let the mind control the equation in the actual execution of the sport or form in question.

When all is said and done, cross-training has its uses. In fact, if nothing else, it gives an athlete or a practitioner a set of options with regards to both technique and training. Within an area as precise as the fighting arts, or an activity as intense as professional sports, options are a great thing to have.

C O N C L U S I O N

Within the constant battle between order and chaos, good and evil, or light and darkness, there is an entity, and that entity is life. We are all living and breathing beings, constantly learning, growing, and changing, not unlike our world, but all these battling elements derive their strengths from constant or solid things. These footholds are what form and shape us into the people we imagine ourselves to be one day.

There are no guarantees in life. No perfect instances where victory or defeat is assured. But should a small handful of rules, guidelines, or experiences be forwarded to be recognized or employed to help others along a similar pathway, then a thread of unity will begin to become evident to all of mankind, a common ground where knowledge and application can be shared. But to reach this stage, we must act as responsible human beings and must look to ourselves and our practices in work, play, hobby, and sport.

With no beginning and no end the martial arts are the perfect principles to call upon to center your life. They can be adapted and improvised to accomodate any and all lifestyles, attitudes, and experiences. For these reasons, you must look to yourself as the teacher of all things. Because, once studied, martial prowess remains a constant until the day we take our final step to heaven.

The path of a martial artist is both long and winding; it is ever-changing and never content with the shape of the world. This rawness to improve or control takes hold of our thoughts and dreams as we grow. Choosing a style in haste, learning from an incompetent instructor, training in a fraudulent school, or ignoring our own inner voices will most surely lead off the chosen path into an area of confusion and utter contempt.

In any aspect of your martial arts journey don't be afraid to be "picky" or "moody"...As my father once told me ...

"Son, though it may seem selfish, and it takes more strength than you might believe, be good to yourself above any and all things. Because after the competition is over, the trophy is won, and the parade has stopped marching, all you have left is yourself...and that's the person that you must live with—today and tomorrow."

Thanks Dad.

"From within one small warrior spreads thoughts and words that will reach hundreds—these hundreds will then utter the very same words reaching thousands— and those thousands then shall cry out these very same thoughts, which will soon encompass the world! What will this small warrior say?"

Glen Doyle

December 14, 1997

Sifu Glen Doyle

The Jing Mo Kung Fu Club
Toronto, Canada

Born in August 1965 in Middle Arm, Newfoundland, Canada, Glen Doyle began his martial arts education at a very young age. His father, Greg Doyle, was a military man who was also a marathon runner and a boxer. Greg Doyle ran for Canada many times and boxed for the Canadian Armed Forces during and after the Korean War.

Greg felt his son would need the education of the fighting arts to help give him confidence and drive. At the tender age of four, Glen put on his first pair of boxing gloves and began his pugilistic career. Under the strict guidance of his father, Glen continued to train for over eight years. However, at age twelve, Glen startled his father with an observation about his fighting art: He told his father that although boxing was an outstanding sport for both endurance and coordination, he found it limited in its realism for street combat. Glen sat his father down and mapped out boxing limits with respect to striking and defending below the waist, and weight disadvantages. In a ring with a referee and a controlled situation, boxing was an incredible art, but Glen, knowing he would not be a large man (his father was only 5' 5" and his mother 4'11"), would be at a disadvantage should he get into a confrontation on the street.

With the support of his father, Glen decided to look for a more complete fighting art. The search took him through a sampling of the Japanese and Korean arts, and even into the military for a few years to test out its hand-to-hand combat program. Nothing seemed to make him feel complete. Then in 1983, strictly by chance, Glen met an elderly Chinese gentleman, Mr. James Lore (Lore King Hong). Lore was a Hung Gar kung-fu teacher at the Jing Mo Kung-Fu Club, which operated out of the Chinese Community Center of Ontario. Glen watched one class and signed up...the partnership had begun.

For the next five years, Glen trained every day for six to seven hours and moved up his club's pecking order. Though Glen was not Chinese, he threw himself totally into both his Hung Gar kung-fu and the Chinese culture and became a recognized face in Toronto's Chinatown, and even got the Chinese name of Lok Siu Fung (after a figure in Chinese mythology).

Glen's next step was the competition circuit, and on his first outing he won the Eastern Canadian Championships and won a chance to compete in the Canadian National Championships, which saw teams from all over Canada and numerous teams from the U.S. The competition was fierce, but Glen emerged as the Canadian Champion, and would keep the title, until he stepped down to pursue other interests in the form of training sports teams and adopting his fighting theories to all aspects of life— from self-defense to self-help.

Developing his now renowned "Stealing the Energy" techniques and theories, Glen went on and became the martial arts coach for figure skating mega-star Elvis Stojko (who still works with him), ice dancers Shae-Lynn Bourne and Victor Kraatz, the Philadelphia Bulldogs Pro-Roller Hockey team, soccer teams, and football teams. Glen's style, flair, and open approach to his martial arts has landed him on the cover of numerous magazines, seen him perform at both national and international events, on television shows throughout Canada and the U.S., and even won him the prestigious honor of being the special guest performer at the historic Opening Ceremonies of the World Wu Shu Championships in 1995, held in Baltimore. It was the first time the games had been held outside Asia, and the event was to be seen by millions via satellite.

Always looking for new ways to spread his teachings, Glen accepted assignments as a fight choreographer for Cynthia

Rothrock and for Canadian film and television programs. This helped him realize his potential to both teach and learn, and Glen began to set aside much of his time to explore this area. Studying film arts and screenwriting at Ryerson University and then journalism at Humber College, Glen developed new creative avenues to increase his power to teach and invent. However, he did not want to stray from the purity of his art, and he still had a drive to continue to educate and help those wishing to better themselves, so Glen decided to put some of his thoughts and ideals into a book form—not to create a picture-filled "how to" book, but rather a simple set of thoughts and suggestions for those wanting to get more from their martial art or sports experiences.